THE BRIDGE BUILDERS

Biographical Studies in the History of Anglicanism

By the same author:

THOMAS KEN, BISHOP AND NON-JUROR
PRAYER BOOK HERITAGE
TO BE A PILGRIM
FOUNDED UPON A ROCK

THE BRIDGE BUILDERS

Biographical Studies in the History of Anglicanism

HUGH A. LAWRENCE RICE

DARTON, LONGMAN & TODD
LONDON

LONGMANS, GREEN & CO INC
NEW YORK

DARTON, LONGMAN & TODD LTD
29a Gloucester Road
London, SW7

LONGMANS, GREEN & CO INC
119 West 40th Street
New York, 18

Printed in Great Britain by
W. & J. Mackay & Co Ltd, Chatham, Kent

CONTENTS

PREFACE

THIS volume does not pretend in any way to be a formal history of the Church of England. There are several such works already available of varying length and merit. All that has been attempted here has been to indicate some of the changes and chances which have marked the progress of Anglicanism over the past four hundred years, as illustrated by pen portraits of some of its leading figures.

There are many worse methods of teaching oneself history than by reading the biographies of the men and women who have helped to make it; there are few better ways of understanding and appreciating the peculiar genius of the Anglican Church and its way of life than by learning something of the great personalities who have shed such lustre on the pages of its past.

The Church of England is sometimes referred to as the 'Bridge Church'—the suggestion being that because of its *via media* doctrinal position it forms a link between the sundry competing denominations, Catholic and Protestant, into which Christendom is so lamentably divided. Since a bridge is something upon which no one remains for very long but which one simply uses as a means of transit from one place to another, the term 'Bridge Church' is not perhaps the happiest of appellations. Nevertheless, inasmuch as the Church of England glories in the fact that she has preserved unbroken the chain of succession with her Catholic and Apostolic past, while rejoicing in her sixteenth-century repudiation of many medieval abuses and doctrinal corruptions, she does stand in a very special relationship to each of the two sides of the ancient Catholic-Protestant controversy and in this particular sense may be said to provide a bridge across what otherwise would appear to be an invincibly separating gulf. It is in this sense that I have referred in my title to the great Anglican Fathers as the 'Bridge Builders' whose name liveth, and whose work abideth, though their bodies have long been buried in peace.

Although this present volume aims at portraying the characteristic genius of Anglicanism as demonstrated by the lives and achievements of a few of its most distinguished adherents, it must not for one moment be assumed that the period covered represents the total existence of *Ecclesia Anglicana*. Nor must it be deduced because the story of *modern* Anglicanism begins with Thomas Cranmer—to whom, amongst many others, it owes so much—that the Church of England was founded either by or in the reign of Henry the Eighth. Nothing, of course, could be further from the truth.

The Church of England has an ancestry reaching back into the pre-Saxon era and an unbroken continuity from the time of St Augustine onwards. Its diocesan and parochial organization it owes to the administrative genius of the seventh century Archbishop of Canterbury, Theodore of Tarsus. Its existence and constitutional rights were recognized and confirmed by the Great Charter, wherein it was laid down that *Ecclesia Anglicana libera sit*. The great cathedrals and ancient parish churches speak of the English Church's Catholic continuity as eloquently and uncompromisingly as so much pre-Reformation legislation testifies to her frequent and stubborn resistance to Papal demands and pretensions. She has preserved intact the unbroken episcopal succession, and in the face of all attempts at doctrinal innovation she has maintained unimpaired the apostolic doctrine of undivided Christendom. Her liturgy and her ways of worship unmistakably proclaim their Catholic origins—a fact which was abundantly recognized and bitterly deplored by the sixteenth and seventeenth century Puritans.

The great names of the past four hundred years of Anglican history are the lawful heirs and successors of Augustine, Paulinus, Oswald, Chad; of Alfred, Dunstan and Aldhelm; of Anselm, Lanfranc, Langton, Becket, Hugh of Lincoln, William of Wykeham, Colet and Stephen Gardiner. It is true that they had learnt to pray in English instead of in Latin, but the prayers they said and the sacraments they administered were Catholic ones. It is true that they had repudiated many medieval accretions and abuses, as Rome herself has done since and is still in process of doing today. The Congregation of Rites is gradually catching up on Cranmer.

The motif of the pages which follow is to illustrate the ethos of the Anglican Church and to vindicate her Catholic claims by contemplating some of the characters and causes which, under God, have made her what she is.

CHAPTER I

THE LAW GIVERS

IN August of the year 1532 old Archbishop Warham of Canterbury passed to his rest, and King Henry VIII nominated as his successor Master Thomas Cranmer, Fellow and Lecturer in Divinity at Jesus College, Cambridge. Behind that appointment there lay a tale of tortuous intrigue; before the new archbishop there stretched a primacy covering twenty-three of the most fateful years in all the long history of the English Church.

Thomas Cranmer was born in 1489, at Aslacton in Nottinghamshire. He was of gentle birth, and suffered in his youth from an excessive timidity which has been attributed to the over-severity of one of his schoolmasters. In spite of this disability, or perhaps by way of compensation for it, he appears to have had the reputation of being an intrepid horseman.

At Cambridge, having been elected Fellow of Jesus, he proceeded to forfeit his Fellowship by injudiciously marrying a young woman who was related to the landlady of the Dolphin Tavern. For a year he lectured at Buckingham College (soon to be refounded as Magdalene), and then his young wife died in giving birth to a child. The impediment of a wife no longer existing, Cranmer was restored to his Fellowship, he resumed his study of theology and in due course he was ordained. As lecturer and examiner in divinity he settled down happily in Cambridge. A long vista of peaceful academic pursuits appeared to lie ahead of him.

This, no doubt, would have been his lot had he lived in any other half-century. As it was he was destined to be drawn into the murky business of the King's projected divorce from Queen

Katharine. Negotiations with the Pope for a decree of nullity had broken down in October 1529, and Cardinal Wolsey, who had been entrusted with the furthering of the 'King's matter', was disgraced. He was ordered to relinquish the Great Seal and was banished to his Arch-diocese of York. He died a few months later, at Leicester Abbey, when on his way to London to face his trial on a charge of treason.

A few months earlier, in the summer of 1529, King Henry visited Waltham Abbey in Essex, accompanied by a considerable retinue. That same summer a plague epidemic had broken out in Cambridge, and Doctor Thomas Cranmer (as he was now) had temporarily deserted his Fellow's quarters and had taken up his residence at Waltham, where he acted as tutor to the two sons of a Mr Cressey. When the royal party arrived in the town, accommodation was taxed to the uttermost, and two important members of the King's entourage, Bishops Gardiner and Fox, were billeted at the house of Mr Cressey. It was a fateful circumstance.

At supper the two prelates met the retiring professor of theology. Talk turned inevitably upon the King's matrimonial problems and soon Cranmer was invited to express his views.

The question of a decree of nullity (which Henry desired, partly to provide himself with the son he was persuaded Katharine was now incapable of bearing, and partly to enable him to marry Anne Boleyn) was by no means a simple, straightforward one. There were several perfectly good precedents for the granting of such a decree, and in the normal order of things the Pope would probably have made no difficulty. It so happened, however, that Pope Clement VII was by no means a free agent. He was virtually the prisoner of the Emperor Charles V, whose imperial forces had recently occupied Rome, and the Emperor was the nephew of Queen Katharine. It was more than the Pope dared do to grant a decree which would deprive the Emperor's aunt of her crown and wifely status and illegitimize her daughter, Mary.

In view of this deadlock Cranmer suggested to Gardiner and Fox that the King's matter might suitably be put to the universities for their opinion, and the two prelates passed on the suggestion to the King. Henry was delighted at the notion. He instructed Cranmer to prepare a brief on the subject and appointed him chaplain to the Earl of Wiltshire, father of Anne Boleyn.

The universities, as it turned out, were not whole-heartedly disposed to reach a finding satisfactory to the King. It was only after much oblique threatening and packing of committees that they could be persuaded to declare Henry's marriage to Katharine to be invalid, and then only on the understanding that the Queen's previous marriage to Henry's brother Arthur had been consummated—a fact which Katharine later strenuously denied.

To consolidate his position, and to abolish the Pope's authority in England, Henry now pressed on with the various anti-papal acts which finally resulted in England's ecclesiastical separation from Rome and the assumption by the King of a quasi-papal supremacy. During the earlier part of this period Cranmer was abroad, actively working on the King's behalf by putting his case before various foreign universities, and even pleading it before the Pope in person. During the course of his peregrinations Cranmer met some of the German princes who had embraced Lutheranism. He also met several leading Lutheran divines—in particular Dr Andreas Osiander, pastor of St Laurence's Church at Nuremberg, whose niece he promptly married. This marriage, of course, was an open defiance of Church law and it is an indication of the direction in which Cranmer's attitude to ecclesiastical authority and discipline was moving. For a priest (or a cardinal such as Wolsey) to take a mistress might be winked at; to contract a formal marriage was to flaunt the colours of open rebellion. It also came near to frustrating Henry's personal plans, for when Warham died in August 1532 the King at once pressed for Cranmer to succeed him. A married priest was still an anomaly and a scandal, but at the thought of a married Archbishop of Canterbury imaginations boggled as violently in England as in Rome. Henry found it necessary to apply all the pressure at his command to obtain from the Pope the requisite Bulls and dispensations.

Cranmer, still abroad, delayed his return as long as possible. He had no desire to exchange the academic calm of Cambridge for the vortex of public affairs which, daily almost, tended to take on a more and more alarming complexion. Eventually when he dared procrastinate no longer, he returned to England about the middle of February 1533. A fortnight or so earlier Henry had been married to Anne Boleyn.

Cranmer was consecrated Archbishop of Canterbury on 30 March 1533, having first made a protest that the oaths of obedience he was forced to take to the Pope would not prejudice him in his loyalty to the King. This act of protest may have salved his conscience at the time, but it proved of no avail at his trial when he stood accused of perjury and oath-breaking. The new archbishop was now required to justify his appointment, and in May he duly pronounced Henry's marriage to Queen Katharine null and void. Five days later he declared the validity of the King's marriage to Anne Boleyn. When the Princess Elizabeth was baptized on 10 September the Archbishop was her godfather.

Meanwhile the clergy of England had been blackmailed into acknowledging the King as 'Supreme Head' of the English Church, and as a consequence Sir Thomas More found himself constrained by conscience to surrender his Chancellorship. The Church in England was now completely under the royal thumb, and though the final, irrevocable breach with Rome had not yet been made, the means of achieving it were within Henry's grasp whenever he desired to make use of it. Yet in spite of it all, the Tudor despot continued to profess himself a dutiful son of the Church. He treasured still the title of *Fidei Defensor* he had once received from Rome for his polemical anti-Lutheran writings. Nor was this hypocrisy on his part. He never ceased to be Catholic in his outlook, never remitted his opposition to Reforming theology, made no pretence of having set up any new Church or any new form of Faith. Tyrant, schismatic, adulterer he might be, but never a heretic.

Parliament, at the King's bidding, now passed an Act of Succession, formally acknowledging the legitimacy of whatever offspring might result from the new royal marriage. All persons of rank and consequence were required to take an oath to maintain the provisions of the Act, and for declining to do so Sir Thomas More and Bishop Fisher of Rochester were sent to the Tower and condemned to death. It is to Cranmer's everlasting credit that he made strenuous but unavailing efforts to save both men from the cruel fate which befell them.

Cranmer seems to have played little part in the royal act of pillage and plunder known as the Dissolution of the Monasteries. His powers of visitation of religious houses had been taken from him by Act of Parliament and, whatever his views may have been, he was compelled to stand helplessly by while one of the most shamelessly cynical acts of spoliation in our national history was perpetrated. There is no reason for assuming that he had any great love for monasticism as such, but there exists a letter of his to Cromwell in which he appears far from happy about the business of wholesale dissolution and the hypocritical way in which the cause of true religion was invoked to justify it.

At Canterbury, it is true, he seems to have accepted without protest, the conversion of the cathedral's ancient monastic structure into the new foundation of a dean and chapter, and in so doing to have incurred considerable local unpopularity. It should be remembered to his credit, however, that he stoutly resisted a determined effort on the part of the King's Commissioners so to reframe the regulations of the King's School as virtually to exclude from it all but gentlemen's sons. He very boldly (for him), and rather surprisingly, asserted that the children of poor parents were better endowed mentally than the sons of the gentry and that they were generally more diligent in their studies—a sweeping generalization and no doubt an erroneous one, but one which at least exhibits Cranmer in a somewhat unaccustomed light.

During the final decade of Henry's reign Cranmer found himself perilously exposed to the proddings of the extreme Reformers on the one hand and the fears of the conservatives on the other. His own sympathies were increasingly with the former whereas the King, having achieved his immediate matrimonial aims and independence of Rome, tended more and more to veto the suggestion of any doctrinal concessions of a Protestant complexion. Heretics continued to be burnt through-out the reign and by the Ten Articles of 1536, promulgated by Royal Injunction, the ancient ceremonies connected with Candlemas, Ash Wednesday, Palm Sunday and Good Friday were ordered to be retained. Confession before a priest, invoca-tion of saints, prayers for the dead and the use of images were likewise commended and endorsed. These injunctions were issued by Cromwell's authority and with Cranmer's acqui-escence, though to what extent either man inwardly approved them is debatable.

The Injunctions were followed in 1537 by a statement of doctrinal belief entitled 'The Institution of a Christian Man' but, since it was mainly the work of Cranmer and Bishop Fox of Hereford, commonly known as 'The Bishops' Book'. This publi-cation, inevitably, was a compromise between the views of the Reforming bishops and divines represented by Cranmer, Hooper, Latimer and Ridley on the one hand, and those of the conservatives such as Gardiner, Tunstall, Heath and Day, on the other. It represents the furthest doctrinal extent to which Henry was prepared to go in a reforming direction.

In 1539 there came the 'Six Articles', in which the scales were tilted in an even more decidedly conservative direction. To those who desired doctrinal innovations the statute embody-ing the 'Six Articles' became known as 'the bloody whip with six strings' because of the harsh penalties prescribed for denial of what the 'Articles' affirmed, namely, the doctrine of transub-stantiation, the necessity of private confession before a priest, the lawfulness of private masses, vows of chastity, communion in one kind and clerical celibacy.

When the statute was debated in the House of Lords, Cranmer and the other Reforming bishops argued strongly against the 'Articles' and the penalties proposed for breach of them. It was only when the King went down to Parliament in person and spoke vehemently in favour of the Measure that the opposition was silenced and the statute passed. Latimer, Bishop of Worcester, and Shaxton, Bishop of Salisbury, at once re-signed their sees. Latimer, already under suspicion of heresy as the result of his denunciations of his brother bishops and the Convocations, was first placed under house arrest in the Bishop of Chichester's Palace and later was incarcerated in the Tower, where he remained until the accession of Edward VI.

Cranmer was once more found ready to acquiesce in legislation against which he had bitterly contended and which was aimed deliberately at the opinions he had come to hold with increasing conviction. Years later he defended himself for his compliance on the ground of the obedience he owed to the King. This Erastian pliability of Cranmer's was a serious flaw in an otherwise not ignoble character, but it may be urged in mitigation that his was essentially a mild, unassertive scholarly disposition, ill-equipped for participating in the ruthless rough and tumble of Tudor ecclesiastical politics. His tragedy was that, admirably suited for a life of scholarly pursuits, he was pitchforked into the surge of public affairs at one of the most disturbed and controversial periods of English history. A Thomas à Becket or a William Laud might have succeeded in riding the whirlwind and directing the storm; Cranmer could only bow before it and find safety in submission.

He should not, however, be judged too harshly on this account. Apart from his defects of character and temperament (to say nothing of his royal master's!), the situation was unfamiliar and imponderable. No one knew for certain that what was lawful today might not be felonious tomorrow; none could guarantee that what was now condemned might not overnight receive the royal support. For those who stopped short of permitting conscience to pilot them to within the shadow of the scaffold, the situation called for no ordinary measure of manoeuvre and adaptability. Moreover, Cranmer may well have consoled himself at this stage with the thought that, while martyrs have their uses in commending a cause, a live archbishop who believed in reform but knew how to bide his time was of more practical value than a dead one who had spoken out too boldly and too soon.

Meanwhile many were required to pay the prescribed penalties for calling in question the contents of the 'Six Articles' and, on the obverse side of the picture, priests and others were put to death for denying the Royal Supremacy. Papists and Lutherans alike groaned beneath the rigours of Henry's ecclesiastical policy while, at the same time, the work of suppressing the religious houses went steadily forward. The King's matrimonial adventures continued to be a source of dissatisfaction to himself and a mortal danger to anyone else unlucky enough to become in any way involved in them. For his part in bringing about Henry's marriage to the unattractive Anne of Cleves—'the Flanders Mare'—Thomas Cromwell was disgraced and finally met the end he had engineered for so many better men. Only Cranmer made any effort to save him, pleading vainly for his life with the implacable Henry.

The fall of Cromwell brought Cranmer, too, within danger of his life. His opponents made determined efforts to have him arraigned on charges of heresy, and only the personal intervention of the King saved him. In Cranmer's case alone does Henry seem to have shown gratitude for faithful service and loyal support in all adversities. A Wolsey, a Thomas More, a Cromwell, might be left naked to their enemies; an erring or no longer wanted wife could expect no mercy; but the man who had gently but none the less surely guided the King along the tortuous path towards unhindered absolutism and independence of Rome would never be abandoned by his unpredictable royal master.

*   *   *

In an age when archbishops, chancellors and even cardinals were held to be expendable, Cranmer was fortunate in contriving to keep his head upon his shoulders through so many perils. It was a fortunate circumstance, too, for English religion, for during the decade that followed Cromwell's fall Cranmer made his greatest contribution to the Church's liturgical development and in so doing contributed notably to the development and enrichment of the national tongue.

Ever since 1534 he had been pressing for an authorized translation of the Bible, and three years later he had persuaded Cromwell to seek the King's permission for the so-called 'Matthew's' Bible (consisting of Tyndale's New Testament and

Coverdale's translation of as much of the Old Testament as Tyndale had not had time to finish) to be sold and read without restraint. It was a far from satisfactory version, containing as it did numerous highly tendentious marginal notes and a prologue to the Epistle to the Romans added to advance the spread of Lutheran ideas. Many of the English bishops justifiably protested, the King's licence was withdrawn only a few months after it had been granted, and Coverdale was instructed to proceed with a fresh translation. The result was the 'Great Bible' of 1539, a copy of which was ordered by Royal Injunction, a year later, to be set up in every parish church. Since it contained a preface written by the Archbishop, this version is sometimes known as 'Cranmer's Bible.'

The introduction of printing in 1476 had, of course, resulted in an ever-rising degree of literacy throughout the country, a fact which enormously strengthened the case of those who were pressing for church services in the common tongue. But, in spite of Cranmer's eager advocacy, the King exhibited once more his innate ecclesiastical conservatism and the innovators were faced with an uphill struggle. The stages by which they eventually achieved their aim of an entirely vernacular liturgy may be briefly summarized.

In 1542 Convocation agreed to an Order directing that a Lesson from the New Testament in English was to be read on every Sunday and Holy Day, in every parish church, after the *Te Deum* at Mattins and after the *Magnificat* at Vespers.

In 1544, at the request of the King, Cranmer compiled a 'Letanie . . . to be said or sung at the tyme of Processyons.' Cranmer's Litany of 1544, based upon the old Sarum Litany of the Saints but with borrowings from Lutheran and Eastern Orthodox sources, is substantially that which appears in our Prayer Book today. It represents the high water mark of Cranmer's literary genius and it provided a magnificent send-off to the liturgical use of the English language.

In 1548, after the death of Henry (professing repentance and sincere attachment to the Catholic faith), came Injunctions requiring that the Epistle and Gospel at High Mass should be read in English and authorizing an 'Order of Communion' to be used in the Latin Mass after the priest's communion. This 'Order' consisted of an exhortation, invitation ('Ye that do truly' etc), a General Confession, Absolution, Comfortable Words and Prayer of Humble Access. Derived partly from ancient sources, partly from Lutheran models, there is little doubt that it was principally the product of Cranmer's compiling and adapting pen.

The scene was now set for a complete translation and simplification of all the Latin service books, and for their compression into one volume. A committee of divines, with the Archbishop as chairman, met to consider proposals which had already been drafted by Cranmer. As a result of their deliberations a Bill of Uniformity was passed by Parliament in January, and received the Royal Assent in March, 1549. The Act not only required that 'the Book of Common Prayer' should come into use by Whit Sunday, 9 June, at the latest, but also imposed severe penalties upon any of the clergy who failed to use it and upon any of the laity who spoke against it. As the official records of Convocation for this period perished in the Great Fire of London in 1666, it is impossible to say for certain whether the book ever received the sanction of the Church's own legislative body.

The principal aims of the committee presided over by Cranmer were four: *Intelligibility*—by translation from Latin into English; *Compression*—by including all the public services of the Church in one book; *Simplification* — by permitting fewer variations; and *Uniformity*—by providing one 'Use' or order of service for the whole realm to take the place of the varying uses, such as those of Salisbury, Hereford, Bangor, York, etc., which had hitherto existed. The main features of the New book were the reduction of the seven Choir Offices of Mattins, Prime, Terce, Sext, None, Vespers and Compline to two—Mattins and Evensong; a drastic reduction of the festivals and saints' days which were to be observed; the 'Supper of the Lord, and the Holy Communion, commonly called the Masse' was to be said audibly throughout, but otherwise very largely followed the traditional order of the old Latin service; the celebrating priest was to wear, as before, a plain white alb with vestments (i.e.

chasuble, maniple and stole) or cope; and wafer bread was to
be used but without any mark or device upon it. Directions
about ceremonial scarcely appear at all, and presumably the
traditional movements, actions and postures of the priest and his
assistants in the sanctuary were to continue unchanged. The
other services of the book were mainly translations from the
Latin Ritual or Pontifical, with additions and modifications of
mainly Lutheran origin.

The Preface to the first English Prayer Book defends its
somewhat drastic simplifications and omissions by protesting,
reasonably enough, that in the old Latin service books it frequently took longer to find out what was to be said than to say
it when it was found. The compilers of the Prayer Book certainly
achieved their aim of resolving the former confusions and complications, but later critics have sometimes complained that in
their zeal Cranmer and his colleagues were not entirely successful in avoiding barrenness and monotony.

The book was duly brought into use, but not altogether with
popular approval for in Devon and Cornwall the people
objected, complaining that the new services were little better
than a children's Christmas game. Their objections, however,
were overruled by the pikes and halberds of the Council's
German mercenaries.

The first English Prayer Book of 1549 professed to be not so
much an innovation in forms of service as a return to what was
believed to be the purer worship of the Primitive Church, so
long overlaid with medieval corruptions and complications. It
was essentially catholic in tone, and consequently was accepted
(though perhaps reluctantly) by the more conservative-minded
of the bishops, such as Gardiner and Tunstall. Although it has
passed through subsequent revisions, enrichments and modifications, it was in its main substance the Prayer Book as we know
it today and as it has been used and loved by generations of
worshippers for over 400 years.

*   *   *

The brief reign of the boy-king, Edward VI saw the religious
trend of the country forced increasingly in the direction of

reform. The cathedrals and parish churches were pillaged of their treasures, shrines and images were desecrated, the chantries were suppressed and their revenues alienated. Foreign preachers and reformers flocked into England, Catholic doctrines and customs were denounced, and in 1552 the Prayer Book was revised in a more Protestant direction. Gardiner and the other bishops who shared his views were imprisoned and deprived.

During the latter part of Edward's reign Cranmer had largely withdrawn himself from active participation in public affairs, but he had on occasion ventured a mild protest at some of Northumberland's more rascally proceedings. When the Protector, casting his covetous eyes upon the revenues of the see of Durham, tried to dispossess the imprisoned Tunstall of his bishopric, Cranmer opposed the passage of the Bill to bring this about. In vain, of course; Northumberland had his way and Tunstall's money as well.

Many of the foreign reformers who came to England at this time, men such as Bucer, Peter Martyr, Ochino and John à Lasco, stayed at Lambeth as Cranmer's guests. They exercised considerable influence upon the Archbishop's theological thinking and upon the Prayer Book revision of 1552. Bucer, in fact, reported to the reforming ministers of Strasbourg that the new (i.e. the 1552) Prayer Book was likely to be 'pretty near what could be wished'.

As a result of these contacts Cranmer's Eucharistic doctrine underwent considerable modification. Whereas in King Henry's reign he had boldly defended the Catholic belief in the Real Presence of our Lord in the Holy Sacrament, ten years later he is found conducting a controversial correspondence on the subject with Bishop Gardiner, who held firmly to the medieval doctrine of the Mass. Cranmer, who had come to believe that the medieval teachings were a corruption of and departure from those of the New Testament and Primitive Church, objected particularly to the custom whereby, although a multiplicity of masses was celebrated whenever and wherever possible, the laity generally received Holy Communion only once or twice a year. He also attacked the theory that the more masses you attended or had said for your soul after death the shorter would be the time you must spend in Purgatory.

Yet although Cranmer's views on the Holy Sacrament were distressing to the more conservative bishops, his insistence upon a reasonable measure of outward reverence in celebrating and communicating vexed and irritated the foreign Protestants. He was adamant that the Sacrament should be received kneeling, in spirited opposition to Hooper, John Knox, à Lasco and the rest, who would have had the revised Prayer Book permit Communion to be taken seated.

The Prayer Book of 1552 and the Forty-two Articles of Religion put out in 1553, probably represent Cranmer's final doctrinal position. He had gone far towards that of the Continental Reformers but he had by no means gone all the way. He clung to the decencies of worship and to a moderate, 'half-way' theological position to an extent which must have exasperated the more radical of his reforming friends. His aim was always reform of abuses rather than religious revolution, and however much some may deplore the concessions he made to the prevailing temper of the times it should be recognized that his conciliatory spirit and diplomatic adroitness was to no small extent responsible for preserving the Church of England from breaking with her catholic past even while she was sloughing off the corruptions of the Middle Ages. No Athanasius he, yet in his quietly obstinate way he builded better than he knew; better, possibly, even than he intended.

*   *   *

It was unfortunate for Cranmer that he allowed himself to be persuaded by Northumberland to put his name to the so-called 'devise' by which the dying Edward was induced to bequeath the Crown of England, quite illegally, to his cousin, the Lady Jane Grey. Cranmer signed under protest; as so often before, when faced with the choice of obedience to his conscience or his King, first registering his protest and then falling submissively into line. When Northumberland's plot failed and the country rallied to the support of the Romanist Mary Tudor, Cranmer to his credit remained at his post, although he can have hoped for little favour from the woman he had helped to wrong. Perhaps he thought there might be some chance of co-existence between those who accepted the Prayer Book on the one hand with those who were bound in loyalty to the Pope and the Latin Mass, on the other. If he did so think he was soon to be disillusioned. For a few months the two Rites existed side by side, the Prayer Book being used in some parishes, the Missal in others. But the Queen, an embittered and unforgiving woman, was merely biding her time. In August 1553 Cranmer was placed under house arrest for his part in signing the document which 'devised' the Crown to Lady Jane Grey. He was never again to experience freedom in this world.

In September he was committed to the Tower on a charge of having spoken against the Latin Mass. In November he, Lady Jane Grey, her husband Lord Guilford Dudley (Northumberland's son), and others were arraigned on charges of high treason. They were found guilty and sentenced to death. For reasons of her own Mary spared Cranmer's life, but Parliament passed a Bill of Attainder involving his deprivation and degradation. In April of the following year 'the late Archbishop of Canterbury', together with Ridley and the aged Bishop Latimer, was taken to Oxford to defend his theological views in open disputation. The result of the debate, of course, was never in doubt, and the three men were kept in prison until such time as it might be convenient to try them formally for heresy.

In the spring of 1555 a determined attempt was made to intimidate all who might hold 'heretical' opinions. Under the ancient statute *De heretico comburendo* Bishop Hooper was burned at the stake in his see city of Gloucester, Bishop Ferrar at St David's and Rowland Taylor in his Suffolk parish of Hadleigh. Gardiner, recently restored to the bishopric of Winchester, was an essentially moderate-minded man and no one suffered in his diocese for his beliefs. Tunstall of Durham similarly discouraged such persecutions. In the diocese of London things were very different, and Bishop Bonner was active in hunting out suspected heretics. During the next three years nearly three hundred persons, most of them obscure, were burned at the stake in London alone. The biggest game were kept for despatch in more academic surroundings. On 16 October, 1555, Latimer and Ridley, after trial before Bishop White of Lincoln, lit their perpetual candle when they were burned to death 'upon the north side of the town (Oxford) in the ditch over against Balliol College.' Cranmer was taken to see them die.

Already, on 12th September, he had been brought to trial in St. Mary's Church before Bishop Brookes of Gloucester, who was assisted by two proctors, representing Queen Mary and Philip of Spain. The charges against him were blasphemy, heresy and unchastity—the latter on account of his marriage. He refused to acknowledge the jurisdiction of a court constituted by authority of a foreign prince (i.e. the Pope), but his objections were disregarded. Bishop Brookes behaved towards Cranmer with respect and courtesy, and his evident desire to persuade the Archbishop to recant and save himself induced him to employ a generosity of speech and promise which probably would not have pleased his implacable sovereign. The two royal proctors showed neither deference nor compassion, referring to the prisoner as a stubborn heretic and a man without conscience. With acute dialectical skill they proved the weaknesses of Cranmer's theological position, particularly where it concerned the Royal Supremacy. No decisions, however, were taken as the proceedings had to be reported to Rome, and meanwhile the Archbishop was kept in prison. There was still some hope that he might be persuaded to accept the authority of Rome. His over-developed sense of loyalty to the temporal power might be invoked to this end since, not only the King and Queen, but also Parliament and Convocation, had now accepted the papal supremacy. Continuous pressure was exercised upon him, and at length, as the Queen had seen fit to do so, he was prevailed upon to sign a document acknowledging the Pope's authority. Having achieved this much, his inquisitors pressed for more explicit admissions.

On 14 February 1556, he was taken to the cathedral church in Oxford and solemnly degraded of his archiepiscopal robes and insignia. Bishops Bonner and Thirlby took from him the priestly vestments, the bishop's crozier and the pallium of a

metropolitan. He was then attired in layman's dress and returned to his prison. Two days later he declared his full acceptance of the doctrines of the Catholic Church, particularly as
touching the Sacrament of the Altar. He abjured those beliefs
he had once professed of a Lutheran or Zwinglian nature, and
proclaimed his belief in the doctrine of purgatory and trans-
substantiation.

If Cranmer ever entertained any real hope that this *volte-face*
would save him he was soon to be disillusioned. His recantation
was at once widely published, but only in order to discredit him
in the public regard. The unhappy old man was induced to sign
yet further and more abject submissions, accusing himself of
responsibility for the schisms and heresies into which his country
had fallen. This self-abasement was likewise unavailing. On
21 March he was brought once more to St Mary's Church
where a platform had been set up for him opposite the pulpit.
It was the day before Passion Sunday. A silent throng filled the
nave and side aisles as the Provost of Eton climbed the pulpit
steps to address them. He explained why Cranmer must die. In
spite of his acceptance of the full Romanist doctrine, and in spite
of the fact that four Reforming bishops had already been burnt,
Bishop Fisher was still insufficiently avenged and only the death
of the Archbishop could completely balance that account. Yet,
since Cranmer had abjured his heresies and once more embraced the fountain of truth, he could rest assured that masses
would be said for his soul in every church in Oxford. Having
thus bleakly comforted him, the Provost then called upon
Cranmer publicly to proclaim his faith.

With tears streaming from his eyes the Archbishop addressed
the congregation. He began by invoking Divine forgiveness for
all his sins, and went on to urge upon his hearers loyal obedience to the Throne, and charity towards each other. As a
statement of his faith he recited the Apostles' Creed.

'And now,' he said, 'I come to the great thing which so
much troubleth my conscience, more than anything that ever I
did or said in my whole life.'

The expectant congregation, the triumphant tribunal,
waited for the solemn denunciation of his former anti-Romanist

views which must surely follow. What, in fact, came next electrified and confounded them.

> I renounce and refuse, as things written with my hand, contrary to the truth which I thought in my heart, and written for fear of death and to save my life, *all bills and papers which I have written or signed with my own hand since my degradation.* And forasmuch as my hand offended, writing contrary to my heart, my hand shall first be punished therefore; for when I come to the fire it shall first be burned.

He attempted to say more, to denounce the pretensions of the Pope, to reassert his former denial of transubstantiation. But his outraged opponents would allow him to speak no further. He was dragged from the platform and from St Mary's Church, to the spot near Balliol College where, a few months earlier, he had seen Latimer and Ridley put to death. Here he knelt in prayer and, after shaking hands with some of the bystanders, prepared himself for the stake. Then, in the words of an eye-witness, 'when the wood was kindled and the fire began to burn, he put his right hand into the flames saying, "This hand hath offended".'

He was tied to the stake, the flaming faggots were piled around him, and 'as soon as the fire got up he was very soon dead, never stirring or crying all the while.'

Thus, courageously, died Thomas Cranmer, a martyr to the beliefs which he had never inwardly denied for all his outward tergiversations. In dying he achieved a nobility and heroism difficult to detect as we contemplate his career as a whole. His subservience to Tudor despotism, his exaltation of secular authority above that of the Church even in matters spiritual, tend to dwarf him in comparison with such forthright predecessors of his in the primatial see as St Dunstan, St Thomas à Becket and Stephen Langton.

Yet he was essentially a good man; irreproachable in his private life, devout and sincere in his religion, gentle and tolerant towards his fellow-men. He alone had interceded on behalf of Fisher, More and Cromwell, had pleaded for the

monks of Zion and had vainly opposed the rapacious Northumberland in his plans of pillage and spoliation. It is true that
at times he seems to have stretched his conscience almost to
breaking point in his desire to please and obey his King, but it
should ever be remembered to his honour that ultimately conscience triumphed over all.

In theology he genuinely sought to return to a purer and
more primitive faith, essentially orthodox yet free from medieval accretions and abuses. And if at times he leaned dangerously towards a Lutheran or Calvinistic interpretation of certain
doctrines, allowance again should be made, not only for the
fact that he was under constant and conflicting pressure from
Rome on the one hand and Geneva on the other, but also that
he was, as it were, the anvil upon which the Anglican *via media*
was in process of being hammered out. He was a pioneer and
made the common mistakes of pioneering. But he laid the
foundations upon which Parker, Jewel, Hooker and the
Caroline divines were able to build to the abiding glory of
English divinity.

Yet it was not in the field of dogmatic theology that Cranmer
achieved his supreme distinction. His legacy to posterity in
general and to the Church of England in particular is undoubtedly the Book of Common Prayer. For over four hundred
years it has provided Anglicans with their *lex orandi*. Whatever
its liturgical imperfections may be (and these, it is now widely
recognized, are neither so numerous nor so serious as once was
thought), its mellifluous and stately prose has stood the test of
centuries, endearing itself to successive generations of church-
goers and providing a worthy framework for Catholic worship
according to the dignified Anglican tradition.

It has justifiably been said that as a compiler of prayers in our
flexible common tongue Cranmer stands in a class by himself,
as surely as Shakespeare stands alone as a poet. No other
Church in Christendom can boast a service-book so beloved of
its adherents; no language has been so enriched by its liturgy as
ours has been by the Bible of Tyndale and Coverdale and by
Cranmer's Book of Common Prayer. Whatever may be said for
or against this man of conflicting loyalties and surprising in-

consistencies, the Liturgy of the Church of England provides him with a memorial of imperishable literary grandeur, and so long as the people of our race continue to worship God according to its stately and sonorous forms the name of Thomas Cranmer will ever be recalled with gratitude, admiration and respect.

*   *   *

While the Elizabethan settlement was principally and perforce a question of a determined defence of episcopacy and a fine insistence upon the decencies of worship, before the Queen's long reign reached its end there appeared the first important statement of the Anglican theological position. The need for such a statement, in the face of Puritan pressure and propaganda, had become increasingly urgent; it was to be fulfilled by one who in perfection of prose closely rivalled Cranmer himself and in clarity of exposition surpassed him.

Richard Hooker, born in 1553 near Exeter, was educated at Exeter Grammar School and then, through the good offices of his fellow-Devonian Bishop Jewel, at Corpus Christi College, Oxford, of which in 1577 he was elected Fellow. At Oxford, Hooker was renowned for his personal piety and ever-deepening scholarship, and after his ordination in 1582 he was appointed one of the preachers at Paul's Cross in London.

Having married his landlady's daughter, Hooker obtained a country living in Buckinghamshire where he settled down to the unexacting duties of a village priest. Not for long, however, for he was soon called from his rustic flock, his modest agricultural pursuits and his study of Horace to become Master of the Temple. Here he found himself in the thick of theological controversy. A lectureship in the Temple Church was held by one of the extremer Puritans, named Walter Travers, whose violently Calvinistic allocutions caused it to be said that 'while the forenoon sermon spake Canterbury, the afternoon lecture spoke Geneva'. Hooker soon became involved in endless wranglings with Travers over doctrine and at last, wearied with such disputes, he applied to Archbishop Whitgift for some less contentious sphere of work wherein he could devote himself to constructive theological thought and writing.

In 1591, accordingly, he was instituted to the benefice of Boscombe near Salisbury, and was made a prebendary. The argumentation with the Puritan Travers had at least compelled Hooker to systematize his dogmatic thoughts and in the more tranquil climate of this Wiltshire parish he was able to concentrate on the task of transferring them to paper. Within eighteen months he had completed the first four books of the *Ecclesiastical Polity* and these were published a year or two later. In 1595 Hooker was presented by the Queen to the living of Bishopsbourne near Canterbury, and here, in 1597, he published the fifth book of the *Polity*. Three years later, on All Souls' Day, he died at the early age of 47.

Apart from Bishop Jewel's anti-papal *Apologia pro Ecclesia Anglicana* (1562), the *Ecclesiastical Polity* is the first major theological work to be written from the specifically Anglican standpoint and the first highly-successful effort to set forth systematically the doctrinal position of the Church of England in contradistinction to those of Rome on the one hand and Geneva on the other. Even so, its depth of scholarship and marked charitableness of tone prompted Pope Clement VIII to declare that it had in it 'such seeds of eternity' that it would 'abide till the last fire shall consume all learning'. It has also been described, by Hallam the historian, as 'the first great original prose work in our language'.

Hooker sought to counteract the destructive tendencies of Puritan polemics with a calmly constructive theology based on reason and natural law. As against those who insisted upon the verbal inerrancy and sufficiency of the Scriptures, Hooker urged the importance of ecclesiastical tradition in establishing those disputed or doubtful points of belief or practice whereon the Scriptures are silent or at the most ambiguous. To him the Church was a corporate society with full powers of autonomy and with authority to decree what its members should be required to believe and practise. The Church of England he proclaims to have complete continuity with the historic Catholic Church of all the Christian centuries. 'To reform

ourselves is not to sever ourselves from the church we were of
before; in the church we were and we are so still'. The Church's
rites, customs and ministerial order, denounced by the Puritans
as the dregs of popery, he defends as dispensations by means of
which the Church down the ages has been guided for the better
fulfilment of her divine mission and vocation.

In his approach to the actual question of the Christian
ministry Hooker tends at times to reflect the generally inadequate conceptions of his age. Episcopacy and the Apostolic
Succession presented themselves to him merely as the best and
most effective form of Church government; it was left to a later
generation of theologians and patristic scholars to appreciate
that in the three-fold ministry of bishop, priest and deacon in
true succession from apostolic times we have an historic,
guaranteed transmission of ministerial authority and sacramental grace. Yet Hooker, while he may have lacked a full
perception of episcopacy as being of the *esse* of the Church, was
in no doubt whatever as to its being of the *bene esse* at least. He
forcefully repudiated the Puritan contention that a Presbyterian
form of Church government accorded most fully with the system
prevailing in the sub-apostolic age. If this were so, he maintains,
it is to say the least peculiar that it should have remained un-
discovered for so many centuries! In spite of all the limitations
deriving from the contemporary climate of thought on this
subject, Hooker's view of episcopacy as 'a sacred regiment,
ordained of God' represents a marked advance upon the less
spiritually exalted Erastianism of Cranmer, as also upon the
drab Calvinistic outlook which Whitgift, for all his insistence
upon decency and order, was never able entirely to discard.

Other aspects of Hooker's teaching further emphasize his
essential conservatism of outlook. It is true that here and there
he employs phrases in connexion with the Sacrament of the
Altar which might be taken to imply a 'receptionist' viewpoint
—that the real presence of Christ is in the worthy communicant
rather than in the Sacrament itself. But here he must be judged
by the general trend of his teaching, and against expressions of
this kind we must set such forthright statements as that in
which he declares that 'the Food of Immortality' is 'a true and

real participation of Christ and of life in His Body and Blood'. Or that in which he affirms that 'these holy mysteries do instrumentally impart unto us, in true and real though mystical manner, the very Person of our Lord Himself, whole, perfect and entire'. Fasting communion he speaks of with approval, while private confession before a priest as 'God's appointed officer and vicegerent' he regards as a desirable preliminary to communion when conscience cannot otherwise be set to rest.

Hooker's firm grasp of Catholic doctrine, his wholehearted adherence to its principles and his lucid exposition of the same undoubtedly preserved the Church of England from embracing a merely negative and destructive protestantism and paved the way for that Church revival on sound traditional lines which was to distinguish the otherwise troubled and disastrous reigns of the Stuart sovereigns. It has been finely said of him that 'his master mind checked and turned the tide of revolution', and that he 'rescued theological controversy from the gutter, investing it with a solemn dignity, richness and grandeur'.

The English Church stands deeply indebted to this learned and humble-minded man, whose dislike of the limelight and distaste for controversy were only exceeded by his lucidity of thought and deep attachment to theological truth.

CHAPTER II

KEEP HONOUR BRIGHT

W HEN, in 1689, William of Orange was offered by Parliament the throne of England a Toleration Act was passed permitting freedom of worship to all who would swear allegiance to the new King. All office holders in Church and State were required to take the Oath of Allegiance or be deprived of their posts. Nine English bishops and 400 priests, together with almost all the Scottish bishops and a large number of the lesser clergy, found themselves conscientiously unable to do so in view of the Oath they had taken to James II, so recently fled to France. They were accordingly deprived and became known as Non-Jurors.

Among those who thus suffered loss of office, home and livelihood for conscience' sake was the highly respected Bishop of Bath and Wells, Thomas Ken. Ken, who thus sacrificially demonstrated his loyalty to his lawful sovereign, as he deemed James to be, had only a few months previously exhibited, in an equally dramatic and fearless way, his opposition to what he sincerely regarded as that same sovereign's unlawful and unconstitutional demands. Ken was one of the 'Seven Bishops' who, sooner than publish in their dioceses James's *Declaration of Indulgence*, suffered imprisonment in the Tower and trial. Their subsequent triumphant acquittal was one of the turning points of English history.

Ken, the son of an attorney of the Court of Common Pleas, was born at Berkhamsted in 1637. His mother died when he was 4 years old and the boy was cared for by his half-sister Anne who was married to none other than Izaak Walton—angler, author and devoted Churchman. At the age of 13 Thomas Ken entered Winchester College as a scholar and left his mark on the place so literally that the visitor to the College cloister may still see, roughly carved on a stone buttress, 'Tho. Ken 1656'.

He passed, in that year, from Winchester to Oxford—first to Hart Hall (later absorbed in Hertford College) and subsequently to New College, that other Wykehamist Foundation where he found a former school friend, Francis Turner, whose future lines were frequently to cross his own. Two other friends Ken made at Oxford were Thomas Thynne, later to become the first Viscount Weymouth, and George Hooper, described by a contemporary as 'the best scholar, the finest gentleman, and would make the best bishop, that was ever educated at Westminster School'.

Little is known about Ken's years at Oxford. They coincided with the closing years of the Commonwealth when the life of the university was still distracted by Puritan domination, the absence of many of the most outstanding teachers because of their Royalist and Anglican sympathies and the official proscription of the services of the Book of Common Prayer. To Ken, whose Anglicanism had been so carefully fostered by the devout Walton and by his schooldays at William of Wykeham's ancient foundation, Commonwealth Oxford must surely have presented a somewhat saddening prospect.

Nevertheless, such is the resilience and optimism of youth, he appears to have extracted what pleasures there were to be had at Oxford of a restrained and sober sort, and his earliest biographer tells us that he had 'an excellent genius for music' and was an accomplished lute player. This love for music never left him and was to prove a solace in later life when adversity overshadowed his paths. Another characteristic which remained with him throughout the years was already noted by Thomas Hearne, the antiquary, who speaking of Ken as an undergraduate says, 'he was, even then, when young, very pious and charitable. He used always to have small money to give away constantly, as he walked the streets, in pence or twopence, or more, at a time as he saw proper objects'. Here we see foreshadowed the bishop who, in his palace at Wells on a Sunday, would share his dinner with 'twelve poor men or women', and when they had dined send them home with what was left of the meal for the use of their families.

The precise date of Ken's ordination is not known, and the first few months of his ministry are likewise unrecorded. It is possible that they were spent at Oxford, perhaps as chaplain of New College of which he had become Fellow. In August 1663, however, Ken was instituted to the Rectory of Little Easton, near Dunmow in Essex, where he entered into a close friendship with the patron of the living, Lord Maynard, and his wife Margaret, each of whom exhibited a noble example of Christian piety.

Ken's stay at Easton was not a long one and during the next few years he became successively Chaplain to Bishop Morley of Winchester, Fellow of Winchester College, Rector of Brightstone in the Isle of Wight, Rector of Woodhay (Hampshire) and Prebendary of Winchester. It was during the latter part of this period, in 1674, that he compiled a *Manual of Prayers* for the use of the boys of Winchester, to the seventh edition of which, in 1700, were added his famous and well-loved hymns—'Awake, my soul, and with the sun', and 'Glory to Thee, my God, this night'. Ken can scarcely be placed in the foremost rank of Christian poets and hymnographers, yet these two familiar hymns, together with an equally lovely though possibly less well-known one, 'Her Virgin eyes saw God Incarnate born' (*English Hymnal* No. 217), are to be found in most modern collections of hymns and will probably be sung as long as worship in the English tongue endures.

In the year 1679 Ken was summoned from the comparative obscurity of Winchester to take his place upon a wider stage. He was appointed Chaplain to the Princess Mary, daughter of James, Duke of York and youthful wife of William, Prince of Orange. The eighteen months which Ken spent at the cheerless court at the Hague were not among the happiest of his life. His royal mistress was a devout Anglican and attended regularly to her religious duties. Her husband, however, morose and dourly Calvinistic, disapproved of the doctrine and sacramental worship in which his wife had been nurtured, and did nothing to make her chaplain's duties easy or pleasant to perform. It was

with considerable relief that Ken, his tour of duty ended, returned to England at the end of the year 1680—but not, however, before he had fearlessly reproached the Prince of Orange
for his ill-humoured and boorish treatment of his wife. He had
also had occasion to stand up to William over the deplorable
behaviour of one of the Prince's courtiers, who had seduced one
of the Princess's Maids of Honour and had proved reluctant to
marry her. William was absent in Amsterdam at the time, and
when he returned to the Hague he found to his fury that Ken
had been instrumental in convincing the evasive lover of his
obligations and that the pair were safely wedded, the customary princely approval having been dispensed with. The
incident, a comparatively trivial one in itself, is indicative of
Ken's outstanding courage, chivalry and sense of justice. These
were qualities which he never failed to exhibit, even when it
was to his own hindrance to do so.

On his return to England Ken was appointed by Charles II
to be one of his Royal Chaplains. This involved preaching from
time to time in the Chapel Royal at Whitehall. It also involved
attendance upon the King whenever he paid one of his frequent
visits to Winchester where Charles, in an attempt to outshine
the 'Sun King', Louis XIV, was building what he intended to
be an English Versailles—a project destined never to be completed. It was on one of these royal visitations that Ken made
his celebrated and spirited refusal to vacate his prebendal
house in order to provide accommodation for the King's con-
cubine, Elinor Gwyn. His refusal might have cost him the royal
favour had the King been anyone but Charles. That easy-going
monarch, however, for all his weaknesses, admired the convictions of others when sincerely held and courageously
expressed and when, a few years later, the bishopric of Bath and
Wells fell vacant, nominated to the post 'little Ken who refused
poor Nelly a lodging'.

*   *   *

Before this came about, however, Ken was to participate in
perhaps the strangest episode of his varied career. In 1683
Parliament decided to evacuate the British garrison of Tangier
and to demolish the harbour and port installations of this North

African town which had accrued to the British Crown as part of the marriage dowry of Charles II's Queen, Catherine of Braganza.

To carry out the demolition and to bring home the garrison of a possession which had become too expensive a luxury for a parsimonious Parliament to maintain, an expedition was fitted out under the command of Lord Dartmouth, son of that 'honest Will Legge' who had helped King Charles I to escape from his captors at Hampton Court. No less a person than Mr Secretary Pepys himself was to accompany the expedition of nine men-of-war and twelve mercantile ships, and Dr Ken was asked to go as chaplain. The great diarist was delighted to discover that one of his sailing companions was to be so eminent a divine, and the two men had much agreeable converse of a theological kind. By way of illustration, Pepys records in that invaluable diary, under *Sunday, 9th August,*

'Up to read by myself some chapters in the Bible; by and by to prayers. This being the day of Thanksgiving for the King's late deliverance, Dr Ken gave us a very good sermon on the duty of subjects to their Prince.'

And under 11*th August*:

'After supper in my Lord's cabin, Dr Ken and I very hot in dispute about Spirits.'

The little fleet arrived at Tangier on 14 September 1683, after five weeks at sea, but it was not until the following February that the work of demolition was completed, and the expedition able to return to England carrying with it the evacuated garrison. The return voyage was a far from pleasant one. Not only did the tiny ships have to fight their way northwards in the teeth of violent gales and mountainous seas, but aboard the *Grafton*, Lord Dartmouth's flagship, Ken and Pepys were forced to endure the company of the odious, foul-mouthed, erstwhile Governor of Tangier, Colonel Kirke. It must have been a profound relief to both men when the *Grafton* at last dropped anchor in Plymouth Sound on Easter Sunday, 30 March.

*   *   *

Ken was nominated to the Bishopric of Bath and Wells on the translation of Dr Peter Mews to Winchester in December 1684, and was consecrated in Lambeth Palace Chapel, by Archbishop Sancroft, on the Feast of the Conversion of St Paul, 25 January 1685. Within a week of becoming a bishop, however Ken was summoned to the bedside of the dying Charles II who had been suddenly stricken down only a day or two before. The easy-going, pleasure-loving king died on 30 January, after belatedly professing his adherence to the Romanist Faith. He was succeeded by his brother James, Duke of York who had never made the slightest secret of his papalist attachments. At his coronation on St George's Day 1685, Ken had the duty of walking beside his new sovereign, under the canopy of state, from Westminster Hall and of standing beside him during the ceremonies in the abbey—a solemn beginning to a brief but fateful relationship.

Scarcely had Ken arrived in his Somersetshire diocese than Monmouth's ill-conceived and ill-conducted rebellion and invasion broke upon the peace of the west country. No sooner had it been crushed with the ruthless cruelty for ever to be associated with the names of Kirke and Jeffreys than Ken found himself once again forced into an undesired prominence—first to plead with the King on behalf of the worthless Monmouth and his wretched rustic dupes; then to minister to the unhappy young man in his condemned cell and to stand beside him on the scaffold as he paid the penalty of his criminal folly.

*   *   *

Back in Somerset, Ken found his rural diocese woefully in need of spiritual leadership and enlightenment. Ignorance of the simplest religious truths was widespread, churches and church services were badly neglected and immorality was rampant. At once he set to work to improve the state of things. As a first step, parochial schools were to be set up wherever possible, so that children might be taught to read, write and say their catechism; the clergy of the diocese were recalled to a realization of their pastoral duties and responsibilities; and Ken began the writing of *The Practice of Divine Love, being an Exposition of the*

Church Catechism. This admirable work, the treatment of which is primarily devotional and only incidentally expository, provides an indication not only of Ken's pastoral love for the souls committed to his care but also of that doctrinal standard from which he never wavered and concerning which he refused to compromise. This may perhaps best be summed up in a passage from this notable piece of Anglican apologetic, in the section dealing with the Church:

> Glory be to Thee, O Lord my God, Who hast made me a member of the particular Church of England, whose faith and government and worship are holy and Catholic and Apostolic, and free from the extremes of irreverence and superstition; and which I firmly believe to be a sound part of Thy Church universal, and which teaches me charity to those who dissent from me; and therefore all love, all glory, be to Thee.

The concluding paragraphs of this *confessio fidei* are typical of Ken's two predominantly characteristic aims—glory and love towards God; charity towards his fellow-men.

The Practice of Divine Love was followed by *Directions for Prayer in the Diocese of Bath and Wells*, a little volume of simple acts of devotion and intercession for the use of the simple folk who comprised the greater part of his flock. At the same time he addressed to the clergy of the diocese, churchwardens and sidesmen a series of *Articles of Visitation and Enquiry* with a view to providing remedies for prevailing abuses. From these *Articles* it is clear that many churches in the diocese were without proper altars, sacred vessels for communion, Prayer Books, Bibles or surplices. Some churches were in serious disrepair, churchyards and parsonages frequently neglected, banns of marriage unpublished, non-residence of the clergy was common, preaching neglected, and the rubrics of the Prayer Book generally ignored. It was little wonder that religion was held in little respect or that a low standard of morals prevailed in country districts.

Ken followed up his literary efforts at improvement by travelling widely throughout the diocese whenever weather and the condition of the roads made this possible. In this way he visited as many parishes as he could—preaching, confirming, catechizing, in many remote parishes and humble places of worship where it is likely no bishop had ever set foot before. This was the kind of personal pastoral contact which ever rejoiced the heart of this true shepherd of souls.

*   *   *

The new King's Romanist proclivities were not long in making themselves felt. With incredible folly, in view of the almost obsessive anti-papalism of the people over whom he ruled, James proceeded to flaunt his faith in the outraged sight of his subjects and to favour his co-religionists at the expense of the established Church of his realm. The Papal Nuncio was received in state at Windsor, Army Officers were dismissed and replaced by Roman Catholics, a Court of Ecclesiastical Commission was created, with vague and undefined powers and Judge Jeffreys of all people, as its president. It was this Commission which suspended Compton, Bishop of London, for failing to discipline one of his clergy who had outspokenly denounced the royal policy. Members of the Royal Household were given the choice of endorsing that policy or relinquishing their posts and among those who preferred to resign rather than be browbeaten was Ken's old friend, Lord Maynard, Comptroller of the Household. Lords Lieutenant of counties who proved similarly unpliable were relieved of their commissions; the President and Fellows of Magdalen College, Oxford, were dismissed and their places filled by the King's Romanist nominees.

The crowning (literally the uncrowning, as it proved) folly of James's Gadarene proceedings was the promulgation of the two Declarations of Indulgence by which the King purported, quite unconstitutionally, to remove all civil and legal disabilities under which Roman Catholic and Nonconformist Dissenters at that time suffered. By the majority of Englishmen these proclamations were seen, not as generous and broad minded efforts to remedy injustices done to minority groups but as an attempt to overthrow the supremacy of Parliament on the part of a dictatorial and high-handed monarch. The constitutional quarrel between King and Parliament which occupies so much of seventeenth century political history, thus entered upon its final and fateful phase; and, as so frequently in past struggles when the rights and liberties of the English people were at stake, no inconsiderable part in the conflict was played by the Bishops of the English Church.

On 25 April 1688, James issued his second Declaration of Indulgence and followed it a few days later with an Order in Council requiring that it should be read in all churches and chapels—in London and within a radius of ten miles on the 20 and 27 May; elsewhere throughout the Kingdom on 3 and 10 June.

The consequences of these two royal actions were immediate and far-reaching. On 12 May Archbishop Sancroft summoned to Lambeth Palace as many of the bishops as could be communicated with and could reach London in time. Among those who obeyed the primate's summons was Ken. The other bishops present were Compton (London), Lake (Chichester), White (Peterborough), Turner (Ely), Lloyd (St Asaph) and Trelawny (Bristol). They proceeded to draft a petition to the King respectfully desiring that their conscientious scruples against having the declaration read in their respective dioceses should be respected. Six of the bishops at once set off by water for Whitehall, the Archbishop, who was already *persona non grata*, remaining at Lambeth.

The events which followed—James's angry reception of the bishops, the public 'leakage' of their petition, their arrest, committal to the Tower on a charge of uttering a seditious libel, trial and subsequent triumphant acquittal—are part of the high drama of English constitutional history imperishably recorded beyond oblivion in Lord Macaulay's hardly impartial but highly memorable prose. If for no other reason, Bishop Ken could incontestably claim his niche in the halls of fame for his share in these dramatic and indeed decisive happenings.

For poor, obstinate, inept, fanatical King James the writing was unmistakably upon the wall. On the very night that London pealed its bells and lit its bonfires to celebrate the bishops' acquittal a message had been sent to the King's nephew,

William of Orange, on behalf of several prominent statesmen and soldiers, inviting the Prince to England to save the country from royal absolutism and papal domination.

Throughout the troubled months that followed—months that saw the incredibly rapid decline in King James's fortunes, the landing of Dutch William in Torbay, the spate of desertions, and finally the King's ignominious flight to France—Ken remained quietly in his diocese, sadly awaiting whatever might be the outcome of these tragic events. Loyal supporter of the monarchy though he was, firmly though he held to the doctrine of non-resistance to the royal will in secular matters, Ken never lost sight of that higher duty to which as a chief pastor of the Church he must ever accord the pre-eminence.

Upon King James's flight and William's occupation of the Palace of Whitehall, Archbishop Sancroft summoned Ken and the other bishops once more to Lambeth. Here they debated at considerable length and in some uncertainty of mind what their future course of action should be. Most of them seemed to be in favour of a Regency, on the grounds that King James had not abdicated his throne. This solution, however, would have involved the legal fiction that James was incapacitated from ruling by reason of physical or mental disability. It is perhaps not surprising that this suggestion should have failed to commend itself to the constitutional lawyers, nor that when, on 22 January 1689, a Convention of the Lords and Commons met at Westminster the proposal for a Regency was defeated by fifty-four votes to fifty-one, Ken voting with the minority. A further resolution, passed some days later, that William and Mary should be declared King and Queen, provoked a protest signed by thirty-seven peers, twelve of them bishops of whom Ken was one. By the middle of February the Convention had completed its business, the Crown had been formally offered to the Prince of Orange, and Ken had left the Palace of Westminster, never to set foot in it again.

*   *   *

With William's usurpation of the throne the days of Ken's career of active usefulness were clearly numbered. In the short period of his episcopate, and indeed for many years previously, he had occupied a position of considerable prominence in public affairs. He had acted as the adviser and confidant of leaders in Church and State, and he was deeply revered for his personal integrity and selfless devotion to duty. Now his conscience was to be subjected to a further searching test and his future fashioned by the relentless unfolding of the pattern of events.

All holders of civil or ecclesiastical office were now required to take an oath of allegiance to the new Sovereign. It is greatly to King William's credit that he tried to have included in the Act for settling the new oaths a clause exempting the bishops from its application. In this he was unsuccessful. The Act was passed on 23 February 1689, and the clergy were required to take the oaths by 1 August at the latest under penalty of deprivation.

The immediate outcome was a spate of pamphlets, letters, sermons from pulpit, press and private pens, arguing for or against taking the oath. Apart from an epistolary brush with Burnet, the Whig bishop of Salisbury, Ken took no part in this public controversy. To him the issue presented itself in no clear-cut, categorical light. He had taken an Oath of Allegiance to James, his heirs and successors, and so long as the line survived he knew where to look for his *de jure* King. Yet no one could deny that William was King *de facto*; could it not be that, for the avoidance of the chaos and peril which might threaten the national life if there were no recognizable leader at the head of affairs, one ought to accept the *fait accompli?*

This was the dilemma in which Ken and a great number of his clerical brethren found themselves. Had no fresh oath been required of them, they might well have felt able to continue in their places. But a fresh oath was demanded and to many the way was made plain. Sancroft, Ken, seven other English bishops, 400 of the parochial clergy, one Irish bishop and practically all the Scottish clergy—bishops and priests— declined to take the Oath of Allegiance to William and were formally sentenced to be deprived of their benefices. Two other English bishops—Lake of Chichester and Thomas of Worcester

—who would also certainly have refused, died before sentence of deprivation could be passed upon them.

So came into being the 'Non-Juror' schism, which was to last for well over a century and which took from the active service of the English Church so many of the ablest and most noble of its sons. These men could ill be spared and the subsequent effect of their departure can be read in the depressing pages of so much of the ecclesiastical history of the eighteenth century.

With his deprivation 'for conscience' sake' Ken's active ministry was over. The remaining twenty years of his life were to be spent in retirement at the great country house of Longleat —the home of his friend of Oxford days, Lord Weymouth.

His actual episcopate had been short in point of actual years, yet so full of events of deepest consequence to the present and future of the English Church and nation. He had played his part and done his duty according to the light as he saw it. His reward, in material reckoning, was loss of position, employment, income, home and the place he had occupied and adorned for so long on the stage of public affairs. Never again did he hold any office or perform any official function, civil or ecclesiastical.

Ken died at Longleat on 19 March 1711, and was buried in the churchyard of the near-by parish of Frome Selwood, as he had requested, 'under the East window of the Chancel, just at sun-rising.'

＊　　　＊　　　＊

The eighteenth century in England, popularly regarded as a period when spiritual things were little thought of and when religion and morals were at a remarkably low ebb, was undoubtedly a materialistic age, an age of comfort and ease and good living—for those who could afford it. The age of Whig ascendancy in politics, and of the social supremacy of the great landowners and country gentry; the age of Palladian mansions and vast estates, of comfortable town houses with their elegant adjuncts; it was also the age of reason and formalism in religion, when anything approaching spiritual vigour and vitality was looked upon with distaste and frowned at as 'enthusiasm'.

Yet, in spite of its prevailing materialism and worldliness, the eighteenth century was not without its witnesses to the things of the Spirit, and among them is to be numbered William Law, a shining and burning light whose warm radiance was in marked contrast with the gloom and chill of so much of contemporary religious thought and practice.

He was born in the year 1686, in the Northamptonshire village of King's Cliffe, some twelve miles from Peterborough. His father, Thomas Law, was the village grocer who somehow or other contrived to educate his son and send him ultimately to Emmanuel College, Cambridge. William was a clever lad and became a good classical scholar. He took his bachelor's degree in 1708 and three years later was ordained and elected Fellow of his College.

Three years after that, in 1714, Queen Anne died and the Hanoverian dynasty succeeded.

> 'When George in pudding time came o'er,
>   And moderate men looked big, Sir,
> My Tory faith I then foreswore
>   And I became a Whig, Sir.'

But William Law was no Vicar of Bray. The Abjuration Oath insisted upon at the accession of King George I would have required him, as holder of a public post worth above five pounds per annum, to deny that the 'Old Pretender', son of James II, had any lawful claim to the English Throne, and rather than violate his conscience in this way he resigned his Fellowship and became a Non-Juror.

His movements during the next few years of his life are obscure, but round about the year 1727 we hear of him living at Putney as private tutor to the family of Mr Edward Gibbon, father of the famous author of *Decline and Fall of the Roman Empire*. Twelve years later, in 1740, Mr Gibbon died and William Law retired to his native village of King's Cliffe. Here he shared a house with two devout ladies—Miss Hester Gibbon, sister of his former employer, and her widowed friend Mrs Hutcheson. Together they devoted themselves to charitable works among the villagers, as well as to spiritual devotion and meditation.

It is said that Law and the two ladies enjoyed a joint income of some £3,000 a year, but only one tenth of this amount was spent upon themselves. The rest was given away. It would appear, however, that their charity was not always as discriminating as it might have been, and its results sometimes met with criticism from the good folk of King's Cliffe—and not least from the rector of the parish, who wrote to Law in the following terms:

> To Mr William Law, Master of Arts,
> Sir,
> It would be unbecoming for me, as a minister of the Christian religion, a religion which above all the faiths which have won the assent and allegiance of men most commends the exercise of charity, to criticize unduly a fellow Christian for his practice of that sublime virtue or to attempt to stem the floods of generous giving.
> I am, however, constrained to bring to your notice the lamentable effect which so much ill-considered and indiscriminate giving must inevitably have in attracting to our locality an inordinate number of idle vagrants, shiftless spongers and incorrigible rogues.
> Nor, I think, should it be overlooked that the exercise of unrestrained charity upon even the needy and deserving may well lead to the weakening of moral effort and to the diminution of that spirit of sturdy independence which are so desirable and necessary if the lower orders of our rural society are to retain their self-respect as well as to rise superior, by their own efforts, to the lowly state to which it hath pleased God to call them.

To which, no doubt, Mr Law would have replied that charity covered a multitude of sins, both in the bestower of it and in its recipients. He might, too, have echoed the sentiment of his famous contemporary, the poet Alexander Pope.

> 'In Faith and Hope the world will disagree,
> But all mankind's concern is Charity.'

In spite of that, however, there was doubtless something to be said for the Rector's point of view. At any rate, protests or not, Law appears to have continued with his works of benevolence, founding in King's Cliffe an institution for the upbringing and education of fourteen destitute girls; while his friend Mrs Hutcheson founded a similar home for eighteen poor boys, as well as caring for four deserving widows.

Law's nineteenth century biographer, Charles Walton, has left us a description of the menage at King's Cliffe.

> Law rose every day at five o'clock, breakfasted on a cup of chocolate, and spent the first hours of the day in prayer and study. At nine o'clock all the household assembled for prayers, of which the psalms and the Collect for the Day invariably formed a part. Law then retired to his room to read, meditate and write, but frequently was he interrupted by the many callers who required spiritual or financial help.
>
> The family dined at twelve in the summer, at one in the winter. Then followed further devotions, after which more reading and writing in the study. Later a break was made while the ladies drank tea, and Law sometimes ate a few raisins. After tea Law went out for a walk, on his return from which he had a light supper with a glass of wine to wash it down. After corporate evening prayers Law retired once more to his study where he smoked a pipe before retiring to bed at nine o'clock.
>
> After the morning service on Wednesdays and Fridays it was their custom to ride out for an airing, Mr Law and Miss Gibbon being on horseback and Mrs Hutcheson with the Honourable the Misses Hutton in their coach.

Such a life may sound singularly uneventful and unproductive according to modern utilitarian standards, but this was far from being the case in reality. William Law is mainly remembered, not for his charitable undertakings nor for his personal piety in an unspiritual age, but for the inspired writings with which he enriched the religious literature, thought and practice of his own and subsequent generations. Those long periods spent in the seclusion of his study at King's Cliffe, those hours of reading, prayer and contemplation, bore their fruit in a crop of writings many of which, it is true, were of merely transient value but one of which, at least, ranked—and still ranks—among the classics of Christian literature.

Law was widely read in the classics and philosophy, was a good French scholar, and had more than a nodding acquaintance with the writings of such contemporary masters of the spiritual life as St François de Sales, Fenelon and Madame Guyon, all of whom, no doubt, influenced to some degree his spiritual development as his prose style was influenced by Swift, Pope, Addison and other contemporary literary giants.

Law became involved, at an early date, in the religious controversies of his time, and notably came into conflict with the tendency, fashionable even among professing Churchmen, to reduce Christianity to a mere code of ethics by rejecting as unnecessary and untrue all its doctrinal and supernatural elements. One of the most eminent of the Latitudinarians, as these protagonists of a reduced Christianity were called, was Benjamin Hoadly, Bishop of Bangor (a diocese, incidentally, he never set foot in), who in a sermon preached before King George I, in 1717, denied the supernatural origin and spiritual authority of the very Church of which he was an ordained and consecrated minister. This sermon, which was widely publicized, provoked from Law the famous *Three Letters to the Bishop of Bangor*, in which he dealt faithfully and conclusively with the Bishop's views. Remark his scathing conclusion:

> You have at once, my Lord, by these doctrines, condemned the Scriptures, the Apostles, their martyred successors, the Church of England, and your own conduct. And you have thereby given us some reason to suspect whether you, who allow of no other Church but what is founded upon sincerity, are yourself really a member of any Church.

Hard hitting, you may perhaps feel, but that was the way in which eighteenth century religious disputes were conducted. The *Three Letters* do at least illustrate the caustic vitality, the irony, the devastating and ruthless logic of Law's controversial style, but it is not because of them that he is remembered and revered today. It is not Law the religious controversialist, but Law the mystic and spiritual teacher to whom Christian thought and Christian literature owe their debt. Law wrote one more major work of controversy in 1732—*The Case of Reason*

—a reply to Tindal's *Christianity As Old as The Creation*, but thereafter he confined himself to loftier and more mystical themes.

He had already published in 1726 a work entitled *A Treatise Of Christian Perfection*, and this was followed three years later by the most famous of all his writings, the *Serious Call To A Devout and Holy Life*. This spiritual masterpiece ranks with the great Christian classics of all time—with St Augustine's *Confessions*, Bunyan's *Pilgrim's Progress*, Pascal's *Pensées*, *The Imitation of Christ* and the writings of St François de Sales. Few religious books have had a more profound or more far-reaching influence. Dr Johnson was deeply moved by it:—

> When at Oxford, I took up Law's *Serious Call to a Holy Life*, expecting to find it a dull book (as such books generally are) and perhaps to laugh at it. But I found Law quite an over-match for me; and this was the first occasion of my thinking in earnest of religion after I became capable of rational enquiry.

John Wesley was also said to have derived his religion in the first place from its effects upon him, and from the first he took Law for his spiritual mentor and guide; while George Whitefield wrote: 'God worked powerfully on my soul by that excellent treatise'. Because of the book's effect upon these two leaders of the new and rapidly expanding Methodist Movement, Bishop Warburton maintained, a trifle maliciously maybe, that William Law was the true begetter of Methodism.

The book had an immediate and, considering the time in which it appeared, most surprising success. It was read and appreciated not merely by the religious-minded. Edward Gibbon, the historian, was not a notably devout man but he eagerly read and deeply admired his old tutor's masterpiece. He said of its author: 'If he finds a spark of piety in his reader's mind, he will soon kindle it to a flame.'

So profound was the impression made upon that careless and worldly age by the publication of *A Serious Call* that many, hitherto heedless of the claims of Christ and Christianity, were led to rearrange and regulate their lives according to its precepts and warnings. The theme of the book, urged with all the

B.B.—D

learning, logic, literary elegance, shrewd observation and subtle irony which its author so abundantly possessed, is the overriding and all-embracing nature of Christianity in its day-to-day claims upon our conduct and our loyalty. By the penetrating way in which it ruthlessly exposes the petty shams and evasions, whereby religion can be (and so frequently is) cheapened, emasculated and rendered impotent, the *Serious Call* provides not only a prophylactic against complacency but also a stimulant to spiritual effort.

And because human nature, with all its vagaries and its needs, changes little from one century to another, the validity of its argument remains unimpaired, and the positive value of its precepts is as great today as when they first appeared in print. Only the slightly archaic style and the conventional (eighteenth century) treatment of the book remind us of the period of its origin. *A Serious Call* possesses the supreme characteristic of the true religious classic in being a book for all Christian and would-be Christian people, at all times, everywhere.

From the chapter which deals with 'Christian Responsibility', for example, we can observe the plain, forceful, incisiveness of the prose style of its author, the practicality of his precepts:

> If self-denial is a condition of salvation, all that would be saved must make it a part of their ordinary life. If humility be a Christian duty, then the common life of a Christian is to be a constant course of humility in all its kinds. If poverty of spirit be necessary, it must be the spirit and temper of every day of our lives. If we are to relieve the naked, the sick and the prisoner, it must be the common charity of our lives, as far as we can render ourselves able to perform it. If we are to love our enemies we must make our common life a visible exercise and demonstration of that love. If content and thankfulness, if the patient bearing of evils be duty to God, they are the duties of every day, and in every circumstance of our lives. If we are to follow Christ, it must be in our common way of spending every day.

To drive home his points Law adopted the device of inventing and describing imaginary characters, providing them at the same time with aptly classical names. For instance, to illustrate how habits can gain the mastery over character he describes a certain lady whom he calls Credula: 'Credula was once a tender mother, friendly and charitable to her neighbours, but now she has become spiteful, malicious, envious, and delights in nothing but scandal'.

He likewise portrays a country clergyman of his time—a thumbnail sketch which, it has been suggested, may even be a self-portrait. 'Ouranios is a country parson who, when he first entered into Holy Orders, had a haughtiness in his temper, a great contempt and disregard for all foolish and unreasonable people; but he has prayed away this spirit'.

Would that we could all 'pray away' the spirit of haughtiness, contempt and disregard! But there were many clergymen in the eighteenth century who measured up to more worldly standards. Of such is Cognatus.

> Cognatus is a sober, regular clergyman of good repute in the world, and well-esteemed in the parish. All his parishioners say he is an honest man, and very notable at making a bargain. The farmers listen to him with great attention when he talks of the properest time of selling corn. He has been for twenty years a diligent observer of the markets, and has raised a considerable fortune by good management.
>
> Cognatus is very orthodox and full of esteem for our English liturgy; and if he has not prayers on Wednesdays and Fridays it is because his predecessor had not used the parish to any such custom.
>
> As he cannot serve both his livings himself he makes it a matter of conscience to keep a sober curate upon one of them, whom he hires to take care of all the souls in the parish at as cheap a rate as a sober man can be procured.

Pope's Dr Arbuthnot could have taught Law very little of the gentle art of damning with faint praise!

Then there is Calidus, the successful businessman:

> Calidus has been so many years constantly increasing his trade and his fortune. Every hour of the day is with him an hour of business . . . he does business all the time that he is rising and has settled many matters before he can get to his counting room. His prayers are a short ejaculation or two, which he never misses

in stormy tempestuous weather, because he has always something or other at sea.

Calidus, too, must have been one of the earliest of those 'blue-domers' who like to speak of 'worshipping in Nature's Cathedral'.

> Calidus will tell you, with great pleasure, that he has been in this hurry for so many years and that it must have killed him long ago, but that it has been a rule with him to get out of town every Saturday and make Sunday a day of quiet and good refreshment in the country.

How recognizable, too, is Law's sketch of Calidus in his attitude to spiritual things.

> If thoughts of religion happen at any time to steal into his head, Calidus contents himself with thinking that he never was a friend to infidels and heretics, that he has always been civil to the minister of the parish, and very often given something to the charity schools.

Then we have Succus, the broad-minded *bon vivant*:

> Succus, if he have at any time a mind to indulge a grave thought, always has recourse to a useful treatise upon the ancient cookery. Succus is an enemy of all party matters, having made it an observation that there is as good eating among the Whigs as amongst the Tories. He talks coolly and moderately upon all subjects, and is as fearful of falling into a passion as of catching cold, being very positive that they are both equally injurious to the stomach.
>
> Succus is very loyal, and as soon as ever he likes any wine he drinks the King's health with all his heart. Nothing could put a rebellious thought into his head—unless he should live to see a proclamation against eating of pheasants' eggs!

The woman of fashion and self-indulgence is held up for our inspection in the likeness of Flavia.

> She has been the wonder of all her friends for her excellent management in making so surprising a figure on so moderate a fortune. She has everything that is in fashion and is in every place where there is any diversion. . . .

She once commended a sermon that was against the pride and vanity of dress, and thought it was very just against Lucinda, whom she takes to be a great deal finer than she need be.

Flavia is the fountain of all the tattle of the town.

If you would know who is rude and ill-natured, who is vain and foppish, who lives too high and who is in debt; if you would know what is the quarrel of a certain house, or who and who are in love; if you would know how late Belinda comes home at night, what clothes she has bought, how she loves compliments, and what a long story she told at such a place; if you would know how cross Lucius is to his wife, what ill-natured things he says to her when nobody hears him; if you would know how they hate one another in their hearts, though they appear so kind in public; you must visit Flavia on the Sunday.

Lastly, let us listen to Law's description of Negotius, the dilettante—the man with the butterfly mind.

Though he always seems to know what he is doing, and has many things in his head which are the motives of his actions, yet he cannot tell you of any one general end of life that he has chosen with deliberation as being truly worthy of all his labours and pains.

* * *

What manner of man was he, this shrewd observer and commentator, this profoundly spiritual product of a mainly materialistic age? There is a stained glass representation of Law in the Chapel of Emmanuel College, Cambridge, erected in 1883; but he always refused to have his portrait painted. An early biographer, Richard Tighe, has, however, left us this brief description of William Law's appearance: 'He was a strong man, broad-shouldered, with ruddy complexion, grey eyes and an open countenance'.

Of the manner of Law's daily life at King's Cliffe we have already heard. It was a life lived in strict conformity with certain fixed rules laid down by Law himself. These rules show us a man to whom worldly power and possessions meant next to nothing, who was content to pass most of his earthly existence in the quiet obscurity of a Northamptonshire village. But the spiritual sweetness he distilled was not wasted in the desert air of King's Cliffe. Its fragrance endures in the deathless pages of the *Serious Call*.

William Law died in April 1761, and with him passed from this earth one of the great figures of English Christianity, and indeed of all Christendom. He was of the salt of the earth when so much of the salt had lost its savour. His light shone forth the more brightly because of the prevailing spiritual gloom. The dry disputations of contemporary divines, the worldly indifference of the well-to-do, the sordid miseries of the poor, led to little regard for religion and fired few with any burning zeal for its promotion. Like our own time, but for mainly other reasons, it was an age not so much of irreligion as of indifference. The rapid progress of knowledge had resulted in an exaggerated respect for the attainments and ability of the unaided human reason, and this in turn seriously affected the current presentation of Christianity. To counteract the rationalizing spirit of the times Christian teachers and preachers were forced on to the defensive, and were mainly concerned to uphold the Faith as an intellectual system to be demonstrated and proved.

It was the peculiar glory of William Law that in an over-intellectual age he stood four-square for the things of the Spirit and by the power of his pen revealed the religion of Jesus Christ, not merely as a dialectical system to be defended, but supremely as a life to be lived.

CHAPTER III

AS THE WATERS COVER THE SEA

THOMAS BRAY was born at Marton in the parish of Chirbury in Shropshire, a village in the valley to the south of the Long Mountain on the extreme western edge of the county, where England merges into Wales and Shropshire's boundaries march with those of Montgomery. The Chirbury parish register shows that he was baptized on the 2 May 1658, so presumably his birth took place earlier in that year.

* * *

As a boy Bray appears to have shown considerable aptitude for study, and after a successful career at Oswestry Grammar School he went up, at the age of 17, to All Souls College, Oxford, and from thence to Hart Hall, incorporated, in 1874 in company with Magdalen Hall, in Hertford College. Here he read widely in theology and took his bachelor's degree in 1678. He would, apparently, have liked to pursue an academic career, but he was precluded from doing this by his parents' inability to provide the necessary funds. He decided instead to take Holy Orders.

The date of his ordination is not known, but in 1679 he was licensed to a curacy near Bridgnorth. He served in that parish for a brief period only, for very soon after going there he was appointed private chaplain to Sir Thomas Price of Park Hall, Warwickshire, who later presented him to the living of Lea Marston, near Coleshill, in the same county. The incumbent of Coleshill, John Kettlewell, was a Non-Juror of saintly life and a devotional writer of some distinction, who had been presented to the benefice by Simon, Lord Digby, on the strength of a

45

reputation acquired from the publication of a book on mystical theology, entitled *The Measure of Christian Obedience*. He and Bray became firm friends.

At Lea Marston, Bray, too, attracted the notice of Lord Digby, principally on account of a sermon he preached at Warwick Assizes, and a cordial friendship sprang up between the priest and the peer. When Lord Digby died he was succeeded by his brother William who presented Bray, first to Over Whitacre in Warwickshire and then, in 1690, to Sheldon, vacant because of the refusal of its incumbent, the Reverend Digby Bull, to take the oath of allegiance to William of Orange.

While he was at Sheldon, Bray began to make a name for himself as a writer, his first published work (issued under the 'authoritative injunctions' of Dr Lloyd, Bishop of Lichfield and Coventry, to whom it was dedicated) bearing the slightly intimidating title of *A Course of Lectures upon the Church Catechism*. In the seventeenth and eighteenth centuries, however, the reading public was not to be deterred either by formidable titles or theological themes and the book appears to have been at once successful. Although only one volume of a projected four was written, a first edition of 3,000 copies was printed and sold and brought him in £700. The work attracted much attention and brought Bray to the notice of Compton, Bishop of London. The latter proceeded to make inquiries about the book's author to whom he subsequently made an offer which was to affect, not only the course of Bray's life and career, but the future history of the Church of England as a world-wide missionary organization.

In 1695, the Governor (Francis Nicholson) and Assembly of the New England colony of Maryland, having decided to establish ecclesiastical parishes and to appoint to them government-maintained ministers, petitioned the Bishop of London (under whose jurisdiction and control all the overseas commitments of the Anglican Church were at that time placed), for a 'superintendent, commissary or suffragan' to set up and organize the new system. The Assembly also petitioned the Crown that the commissary, when appointed, should be given judicial powers; but here a difficulty arose in that Lord Baltimore, the 'proprietor' of Maryland, had full and sole authority to establish courts, appoint rules of procedure and select judges.[1]

Apparently the Crown was unwilling to ask Lord Baltimore to relinquish the rights granted by King Charles I and Compton proceeded to appoint Bray as commissary, ignoring the Assembly's request that he should be granted judicial powers. The appointment was made in April 1696, but Bray's departure for the Church in Maryland had still to receive the royal assent which, owing to a defective clause, it failed to do. This necessitated the drafting of a new Act and while this was going forward Bray occupied himself with seeking recruits for Maryland parishes, for in 1696 there were only eight Anglican clergymen resident in the colony. In December 1696, at the repeated request of Governor Nicholson, Bray took the Oxford degrees of Bachelor and Doctor of Divinity although he could ill-afford to do so. The emoluments of the post of commissary were said to be £400 per annum but no payment was made to him during the period of his forced partial inactivity, and through being unable to complete his 'Catechetical Lectures' he must have incurred considerable financial loss.

Whilst waiting for matters in Maryland to be straightened out and while recruiting men for parochial work in the colony, Bray discovered that most of those who offered themselves were too poor to purchase books; whereupon he drew up a report to the bishops in England stressing the urgent need for the foundation of libraries for the use of the clergy, and also for the encouragement of academic and scholarly tastes amongst the men who were to minister in the colonies. He made it abundantly clear that he would be willing to go to Maryland only if the bishops would help to provide such libraries, for the use of

[1]Maryland was named in honour of Henrietta Maria, queen consort of King Charles I. It had been founded under royal charter, by the first Lord Baltimore as a colony for Romanist recusants and its 'proprietor' was given practically royal powers. In 1649 the Assembly had passed an Act of Toleration granting freedom of worship to all Christians, whatever their denomination. This liberal measure provoked the Puritans living in the colony to rebellion and in 1652 Commissioners of the English Cromwellian government seized control. After the Restoration, however, the second Lord Baltimore resumed his inherited powers and prerogatives, and maintained them until 1692 when, once more, they passed under government control.

priests at home as well as overseas. This report was well received and on being assured of episcopal support Bray went ahead with his plans.

He had conceived the idea of establishing parochial libraries in every deanery throughout England and Wales, as well as in the colonies of Maryland and Virginia, and to make his project more widely known he published, in 1697, *An Essay Towards Promoting All Necessary and Useful Knowledge, Both Divine and Human, In All Parts Of His Majesty's Dominions*. The libraries were not to be exclusively clerical.

'For our younger gentry,' he wrote,

> I cannot but think it would tend extremely to furnish their minds with useful knowledge as well as render them serviceable to their families and countries, and will make them considerable both at home and abroad, and will keep them from idle conversation and the debaucheries attending it, to have choice collections of such books dispersed thro' all the Kingdom, and waiting upon them in their own parlours, as will ennoble their minds with principles of virtue and true honour, and will file off that roughness, ferity and barbarity which are the never-failing fruits of ignorance and illiterature.

But if the libraries were to be available to the laity as well as to the clergy their contents were not to be secular or frivolous.

> The truth is, there are a sort of writers which are traditionally handed down from one old study to another, who are not such a good-humoured and inviting society as to make one delight much in their conversation. But what man of spirit or education, had he a Justin Martyr, a Tertullian or Cyprian; a Sanderson, a Hammond or a Tillotson come to visit him, would leave such men of sense for the Society of the sons of Belial ?'

This work was soon followed by two further products of Bray's prolific pen—*Apostolick Charity*, in which he aimed at raising the standard of missionary and colonial pastoral work; and *Bibliotheca Parochialis* designed to give further impetus to his cherished project of parochial libraries.

So well, in fact, did this plan succeed that before his death Bray had brought into being more than eighty libraries in

Britain and thirty-nine in the North American colonies. His first overseas library was set up in Annapolis,[1] the new capital of Maryland. Sir Thomas Lawrence, Secretary of Maryland, went with Bray to wait upon the Princess in order to seek her consent to the town's rechristening. When she heard of Bray's library scheme she immediately expressed her distinguished approval and gave a generous donation. This Annapolis foundation was the first lending library in any of the British colonies and was for long the largest collection of books in America. Many of the original volumes are still in the possession of St John's College, Annapolis. Other libraries were set up at Boston, New York, Charleston, East Jersey and elsewhere. Over 33,000 tracts and books were sent to America—no small feat in those days of limiting printing press output and hazardous transportage. The first thirty libraries founded by Bray in Americal cost the remarkably economic sum of £2,000, of which £1,500 was subscribed and the remainder contributed by Bray himself.

All this time he was apparently receiving no stipend as commissary, and some time later he wrote—'I have spent three full years and upwards in the carrying on of this Design solely at my own Charge and have undergone an unspeakable Labour and Fatigue in the prosecution thereof'. He was offered, during this period, the benefice of St Botolph, Aldgate, but he refused to abandon his mission to Maryland.

★   ★   ★

While working on his library project Bray conceived a far-reaching idea for the more effectual propagation of Christianity in the colonies. His opportunity seemed to have come when, in 1697, a Bill was introduced into Parliament to alienate lands 'given to superstitious uses' and to vest them in the Greenwich Hospital. Bray petitioned that a share of the proceeds should be vested in a corporation for 'The Propagation of True Religion in the Foreign Plantations' but failed to carry his point. In the following year he petitioned for the grant of some arrears of

[1]At first known as Ann Arundel and subsequently renamed out of compliment to the future Queen Anne.

taxes due to the Crown. This petition was more favourably
received than the first, but to complete the grant he was forced
to journey to Holland (where King William then was) in order
to obtain the royal sign manual. Unfortunately the recovery of
the monies proved so difficult that the grant was virtually
worthless.

While at The Hague, however, Bray made the acquaintance
of the King's secretary, Abel Tassin, Sieur D'Allone, who was
so struck by Bray's zeal in the cause of Christian education and
missionary enterprise that he gave him sums of money amount-
ing to £900 and bequeathed by will to Dr Bray and his associates one-tenth of his estate in England as well as arrears of
pension due to him from the Crown. This gift, with £500 from
another well-wisher, the Reverend Abbot Upcher, forms the
capital of a trust fund still administered by 'Dr Bray's Associates' for the assistance of Negro schools in the Bahamas.

Meanwhile, his great plan of a society for the propagation of
Christianity at home and abroad still occupied Bray's mind,
and soon after his return from Holland he drafted the outline
of a scheme for such a body, which he proposed should be incorporated under royal charter. The original draft, of which
there are four copies in the library of Sion College, is entitled:
*A General Plan for the Constitution of a Protestant Congregation or
Society for Propagating Christian Knowledge.*

In this draft it was laid down that the Society should consist
of both clergy and laymen, that it should be incorporated by
Royal Charter and that it should, as and when necessary, meet
and consult as to the best means of achieving the objects at
which it aimed. Its overseas work would be to provide and
support missionaries for 'the Plantations', to provide libraries
for their use, to allot gratuities and pensions to missionaries who
had rendered meritorious service, and to make provision for
widows and orphans of those missionaries unable themselves to
provide for their families. At home 'Catechetical Libraries' were
to be inaugurated for the use of the clergy in the smaller
parishes and market towns; 'Catechetical Schools' were to be
set up for the education of poor children in reading and writing
and in the principles of the Christian Faith; while it was pro-

posed that the Congregation *pro Propaganda Fide* be empowered to receive gifts, grants and legacies to enable it to fulfil the purposes of its foundation.

The scheme, as drawn up by Dr Bray, received strong support from Bishop Compton but no immediate official action was found feasible. The upshot, however, was the formation on a voluntary basis of a 'Society for the Promoting of Christian Knowledge'. This took place on 8 March 1699, at a meeting held at the house of Mr Justice Hooke. In addition to Hooke himself, there were present Bray; Francis, Lord Guilford; Sir Humphrey Mackworth, M.P. (of Betton Grange, Shropshire), and Colonel Maynard Colchester, M.P. A month later John Chamberlayne, a distinguished scholar and linguist, became first a member and then secretary to the new Society; and, later, first secretary of its daughter organization, the Society for the Propagation of the Gospel (S.P.G.). The foundation members of the S.P.C.K. were thus all men of experience and standing— 'rich men furnished with ability', except for Bray, who had the ability without the riches.

At the Society's first meeting it was decided that inquiries should be made as to the prospects of winning Quakers to Anglicanism, to consider the provision of catechetical schools in and around London, and to ask Archbishop Tenison to have inserted in a Bill then before parliament a clause providing that instruction in reading and in the Catechism should be given to children, and that a scheme drawn up by Bray for promoting religion in the colonies should be laid before the Society.

This last decision proved to be of vital importance as it led to the formation, three years later and after Bray's return from Maryland, of the 'Society for the Propagation of the Gospel in Foreign Parts'.

*   *   *

The original aims of S.P.C.K. were many and varied, and included a campaign for improving the tone of contemporary stage plays and the theatre in general, as well as the extirpation of profanity—especially amongst sailors. At a meeting held on 10 March 1701, it was resolved

That Sir John Phillips (a prominent member of S.P.C.K.) be desired to speak to Sir George Rooke (he who in 1704 captured Gibraltar) about dispersing (i.e. distributing) the *Seaman's Monitor*, together with *A Kind Caution Against Swearing* and a *Persuasive to the Observation of the Lord's Day amongst the saylors of his Majesty's Navy*.

And on 14 July in the same year it was resolved that 'The Secretary doe write to Mr. Hodges, Chaplain Generall of the Fleet, about the method of dispersing the Society's Books and Papers amongst the Seamen'.

Within a few months of its formation the Society was strengthened by the accession to its ranks of many bishops and other notable persons; possibly the best-known amongst the former being Gilbert Burnet, Bishop of Salisbury, and the saintly Thomas Wilson, Bishop of Sodor and Man; amongst the lay recruits, Robert Nelson, Non-Juror, religious writer and philanthropist.

★   ★   ★

Meanwhile, a second Act for establishing the Anglican Church in Maryland had shared the fate of its predecessor, mainly because it contained a clause erroneously declaring all the laws of England to be in force in the colony.[1] Bray at once wrote to the Maryland Assembly urging revision and re-enactment of the Bill. He had already waited for two years and was anxious to pay his visit to the colony in his capacity as commissary.

Bray had married for the second time in 1698 and it was about this time that, as already mentioned, he was offered the benefice of St Botolph, Aldgate, some of his friends urging him to accept preferment rather than continue to act as commissary without remuneration. Bray, however, was set on going to America and refused the living, although he was obliged to sell various personal possessions to raise the necessary funds for his passage.

He embarked at Gravesend on 16 December 1699, his ship

[1] This clause was, in fact, *ultra vires*, in that it went beyond the provisions of the Act to establish the Church.

reaching Deal on the twentieth of the same month. The next day it sailed for Plymouth, arriving there on Christmas Eve and anchoring until the 4 January. Bray spent the intervening time ashore and with characteristic zeal seized the opportunity, as indeed he had done at Gravesend and Deal, of establishing libraries and depositing books for the use of missionaries, naval chaplains and other clerics who might find themselves in these ports, delayed on their journeys or awaiting passages, and who might otherwise be tempted to 'saunter away whole hours together in Coffee Houses or maybe less sober places'.

Bray's ship reached Maryland on 12 March and his first act on arrival was to call on the Governor, Colonel Nathaniel Blakiston, who had succeeded Francis Nicholson on the latter's appointment to the governorship of Virginia. Bray brought a letter of introduction from Archbishop Tenison to which the Governor wrote a courteous and respectful reply, pointing out the difficulties which had arisen through the failure of the Establishment Act to receive the royal assent—a circumstance which he attributed in no small degree (and correctly as it subsequently transpired) to the anti-Anglican manœuvrings on the part of the Quaker sect, both at home and in the Colony.

The Assembly was due to meet in May, and in the interval Bray occupied himself with obtaining all the information he could concerning matters ecclesiastical in the colony. He discovered that a large proportion of the population was nominally Anglican, about one-twelfth was Roman Catholic and a slightly higher proportion was of the Quaker persuasion. During this period Bray also preached several sermons and performed sundry other duties pertaining to his priestly office.

He and the Maryland Attorney-General were entrusted with the main part of the task of redrafting the Establishment Act, and Bray's influence upon members of the Assembly probably did much to ensure the passing of the Act.[1] How far he was responsible for the insertion of a clause laying it down that 'The Book of Common Prayer and Administration of the

[1]There is, at Sion College, an interesting list of all the members of the Council and Assembly, with notes upon their views and probable votes, given to Bray by Speaker Smithson.

Sacraments with the Rites and Ceremonies of the Church, according to the Use of the Church of England . . . be solemnly read by all and every Minister or Lay Reader in every Church *or other place of Publick Worship* within this Province' it is hard to say. Such a requirement, clearly contrary not only to the principle of liberty of conscience but also to the statutes of Maryland guaranteeing freedom of worship to all religious denominations, was bound to arouse indignant hostility and opposition on the part of Quakers and Roman Catholics. So illiberal and unrealistic an enactment would have been less characteristic of Bray than of the former Governor Nicholson, who was known to be a bitter opponent of all dissenting bodies and who had returned to Annapolis to consult with Bray and Blakiston and to help them to get the Act through the Assembly. It may well be that it was he who insisted upon the insertion of the clause.

On 7 May the Act passed *nem. con.* and a vote of thanks to Bray was passed by the Assembly for his advice and help in preparing the Measure. He was then asked by the Assembly to solicit the aid of Archbishop Tenison and Bishop Compton in securing the Royal Assent to the Act, and it was suggested that to this end he should return to England as soon as he conveniently could. This he agreed to do, but before he left he summoned the clergy of Maryland to meet him at a general visitation to be held at Annapolis on 22 May 1700. The purpose of this visitation he declared to be:

1. 'To prevent scandals in the Ministers who should come in;[1]
2. To keep them in their duty of Catechising, Preaching and Teaching;

and

3. To propagate the true Religion in the neighbouring Provinces.'

Seventeen members of the Maryland clergy appeared in answer to Bray's summons to the visitation and listened to a

[1]A very 'scandalous minister' had come over in the same ship as Bray—to his great concern.

charge in which he characteristically laid stress first of all on the instruction of children. He then warned his hearers not to give any clergyman a charge unless he had a good character from the ship he came out in; 'whether in his whole passage he gave no manner of scandal, and whether he did constantly read prayers twice a day and catechize and preach on Sundays, which, notwithstanding the common excuses, I know can be done by a minister of any zeal for religion.'

Unfortunately, the clergy received their appointments from London and it is not easy to see how the local clergy were to prevent a scandalous cleric from taking up a living, as in fact such men quite frequently did. Bray, however, had only one such to deal with; a certain 'Mr T—' who had married in Maryland, there being 'violent presumptions that Mr T— had a wife in England'. Mr T— admitted that there had been a lady, but denied that he had married her.

We learn also from resolutions passed by the clergy, that there was a serious shortage of ordained ministers—'there being very many clergy wanting to supply the vacant parishes'.[1] We also learn that the quality of those who came was not always good. At least, the signatories say that it is 'of the greatest consequence that they should be the best chosen'. They had hoped 'his Reverence', as they styled Dr Bray, 'would return with them and so may the better know their behaviour at sea'.

In addition to these measures for supporting and increasing missionary endeavour, proposals were put forward for 'the Propagation of the Christian Religion and for the reduction of the Quakers thereunto in the Province of Pennsylvania'. To this end a subscription was opened and headed by Bray with a donation of £10. Other subjects dealt with, at what appears to

---

[1]After 1703, when the S.P.G. fixed on the Reverend Thorowgood Moore 'to be their missionary to the Indians bordering on New York', that Society upheld the banner of episcopacy in America. During a period of seventy-five years it maintained more than three hundred ordained missionaries whose business was to convert the Indians and Negro slaves, and to minister to the settlers. John Wesley was, for a time, one of the missionaries. They penetrated to New England, and by 1730 there were four episcopal churches in Rhode Island and three in Massachusetts. There were working in New York province the minister of Trinity Church and ten S.P.G. missionaries.

(C. P. S. Clarke—*A Short History of the Christian Church*, pp. 471–2.)

have been a kind of diocesan synod without a bishop, were
religious teaching for children in the province and the inauguration of a 'Scheme of Divinity' by means of which sermons could
be preached on the 'Duties of Magistrates, and against
Prophaneness and Immorality'.

On the third and last day of the visitation, Bray was urged
by the clergy of the colony to return to England forthwith to
seek the Royal Assent to the Act of Establishment, a procedure
which they felt would be even more productive of good for the
Church in Maryland than Bray's continued presence in the
colony. Having indicated his agreement and having arranged
for the convoking of subsequent visitations, Bray brought the
proceedings to a close. Soon afterwards he sailed for England,
taking with him the Act requiring the King's Assent.

On arriving in this country, however, he found that the
Quakers had been busy in his absence organizing strong opposition to the Act, and in spite of a pamphlet which Bray at once
wrote and published on *The Present State of Religion on the Con-
tinent of North America* and in which he powerfully refuted their
contentions, the Act failed yet once more to receive the necessary
sanction. The measure was not, however, rejected outright. Bray
was authorized to amend it and so, with characteristic fortitude
he set himself to the task of redrafting a new Bill for which at
last, after three more attempts, he secured the approval of the
Lords of Trade. This revised Act was sent to Maryland, was
passed unaltered by the Assembly and was returned to England
once more for the King's approval. William III and his advisers
being at last satisfied that toleration would be extended to
Quakers in the Colony, the Royal Assent was duly forthcoming.

Under the new Act, in which liberty of worship was safe-
guarded for Quakers and other dissenters, every Anglican
congregation was to be deemed an integral part of the established Church and the raising of revenue for the maintenance
of ministers provided for. It was further enacted that each
parish should have a vestry of not fewer than six members, the
incumbent in each case to be the chairman. Furthermore, every
minister 'presented, inducted or appointed' by the Governor
was to receive 40 lb of tobacco per head as his emolument, out

of which he was to pay 1,000 lb yearly to a parish clerk! The measure remained in force throughout Maryland's colonial history—a worthy memorial to Bray's persistence and zeal.

The Act safely passed, Bray dispatched several circular letters to the clergy of Maryland on the subject of his recent visitation and 'to enforce such Resolutions as were taken therein'. These letters clearly indicate that Bray intended to return to America, but foreseeing that this would not be possible for some considerable time he deputed some of the senior priests of the province to act for him, to convene gatherings of the clergy, to visit the several parishes, libraries and churches, and to issue such instructions as he might from time to time send them. Owing, however, to his subsequent preoccupation with a project of more compelling urgency and greater moment the opportunity for Bray to return to Maryland did not, in fact, occur.

This project was no less an undertaking than the founding of one of the most valuable and revered of Anglican institutions—that which is familiarly and affectionately known by its initials —S.P.G. It will be remembered that Bray had earlier conceived an ambitious plan for the formation of a chartered missionary society, but this having for various reasons proved impracticable he now decided that a department of the rapidly developing S.P.C.K. might well be devoted to this particular purpose.

When this new plan was made known support was at once forthcoming from Archbishop Tenison and Bishop Compton, and on 13 March 1701, the Lower House of Convocation appointed a committee to 'inquire into ways and means for Promoting Christian Religion in our Foreign Plantations'. Two days later this committee, with commendable celerity, met for the first time and not long afterwards Bray drew up a petition to the King in the following terms:

> To the King's Most Excellent Majesty, the humble Petition of Thomas Bray, D.D., Humbly sheweth That the Numbers of the Inhabitants of your Majesty's Provinces in America have of late years greatly increased; that in many of the Colonies thereof, more especially on the Continent, they are in very much Want

of Instruction in the Christian Religion and in some of them utterly destitute of the same, they not being able to raise a sufficient Maintenance for an Orthodox Clergy to live amongst them, and to make such other Provision, as shall be necessary for the Propagation of the Gospel in those Parts.

Your Petitioner further sheweth, That upon his late arrival into England from thence, and his making known the aforesaid matters in this City and Kingdom, he hath great Reason to believe, that many Persons would contribute, as well by Legacy as by Gift, if there were any Body Corporate and of Perpetual Succession now in being and established in this Kingdom, proper for the Lodging of the said Legacies and Grants therein.

Now forasmuch as your Majesty hath already been graciously pleased to take the State of the Souls of your Majesty's Subjects in those Parts so far into Consideration, as to found and endow a Royal College in Virginia for the Religious Education of their Youth; Your Petitioner is thereby the more encouraged to hope that Your Majesty will also favour any the like Designs and Ends which shall be Prosecuted by proper and effectual means.

Your Petitioner, therefore, who has lately been among Your Majesty's Subjects aforesaid, and has seen their Wants and knows their Desires, is the more emboldened, humbly to request that Your Majesty would be graciously pleased to issue Letters Patent, to such Persons as Your Majesty shall think fit, thereby Constituting them a Body Politick and Corporate, and to grant them and their Successors such Powers, Privileges, and Immunities as Your Majesty in great Wisdom shall think meet and necessary for the Effecting the aforesaid Ends and Designs.

And Your Petitioner shall ever Pray, etc.

Thomas Bray.

This orotund document, with its plethora of punctuation marks and its superfluity of capital letters, was duly acknowledged by James Vernon, the King's Secretary of State, in a memorandum dated 'Whitehall, April 4th, 1701', which promised that it should be referred to the Attorney-General or Solicitor-General, upon receipt of whose opinion King William would make known his further pleasure.

Bray promptly drafted a charter for the proposed society and this was read at a meeting of the S.P.C.K. held on 5 May.

At a further meeting, held a week later, his Petition to the King was read, together with 'other Papers relating to the Corporation to be erected for the Propagation of the Gospel in Foreign Parts', and Archbishop Tenison forthwith promised a subscription of 20 guineas towards the cost of obtaining the Charter. On 19 May the draft of the Charter was again read, several amendments were made to it, and the names of the secretary and other officials of the new society were formally proposed and adopted. The Charter received the royal approbation and on the 16 June the Great Seal of England was affixed to it, thereby bringing into legal being the 'Society for the Propagation of the Gospel in Foreign Parts'.

At the next meeting of S.P.C.K., held on the 23 June, the Charter was read by Bray and it was resolved that the thanks of the Society should be extended to him for 'his great Care and Pains in procuring the Grant of the said Letters Patent'. A committee, of which Bray was to be a member, was then appointed to ascertain from the Archbishop (named in the Charter as the first president of S.P.G.) when and where he wished the first meeting of the new Society to be held. It was provided in the Charter that the two archbishops, the Bishops of London and Ely, the Lord Almoner, the Deans of Westminster and St Paul's, the Archdeacon of London, and the two Regius and Lady Margaret Professors of Divinity at Oxford and Cambridge should always be members of the Society.

The first meeting of S.P.G. took place at Lambeth Palace on 27 June, and the second on 8 July 1701, when the standing orders and bye-laws were passed providing, amongst other things, that an annual sermon should be preached before the Society, that the Seal of the Society should be 'A Ship under Sail, making towards a Point of Land, upon the Prow standing a Minister with an open Bible in his hand, People standing on the shore in a posture of Expectation, and using the words: *Transiens Adjuva Nos*',[1] and that the Motto round the Seal should be *Sigillum Societatis de Promovendo Evangelio in Partibus Transmarinis.*[2]

[1]'Come over and help us', vide Acts. Ch. xvi. 9.
[2]'Seal of the Society for the Propagation of the Gospel in Foreign Parts.'

The Seal and Motto of S.P.G. have remained the same for 250 years and are known today wherever the Anglican Church has taken the Christian message, even unto the uttermost parts of the earth.

Bray was still deeply concerned with the shortage of suitable books for the use of the parochial clergy and in 1702 he published his *Bibliotheca Catechetica* or 'The Country Curate's Library', and in the following year a tract entitled 'The Whole Course of Catechetical Instruction,' both of which works were intended to draw public attention to the need of which he was so acutely conscious. In spite of their formidable titles and no doubt equally formidable appearance, these publications had a ready sale and it was largely owing to their effect upon the minds of prominent readers of them that in 1708 an Act of Parliament 'For the Better Preservation of Parochial Libraries in that part of Great Britain called England' was sponsored by Sir Peter King, Recorder of London and afterwards Lord Chancellor and first Baron King of Ockham.

*   *   *

By 1703 Bray had given up his original intention of returning to Maryland and consequently he asked Bishop Compton to appoint another commissary in his place. The Bishop's choice fell upon the Archdeacon of Armagh, Michael Huitsson[1] who, 'out of pure zeal to the work of Propagating the Gospel in Foreign Parts, was very willing to bestow himself upon that service.'

There had recently been a case where a clergyman, deprived of his benefice in Virginia for unseemly conduct, had been nominated by the Governor to a living in Maryland. To ensure that there should be no repetition of this procedure, Bray proposed to Compton that the new commissary should possess the power of induction and that the Governor should retain the right of presentation only. The Bishop agreed to this suggestion and further proposed that the commissary should also be given judicial authority in matters concerning probate of wills. To win the support and approval of the Governor,

[1]Or Hewetson.

Colonel John Seymour, Compton invited him to meet Bray and Huitsson at dinner at Fulham Palace. The proposition, however, would not appear to have pleased His Excellency for as he was being driven home in the same coach as the two clerics he furiously upbraided them for their part in the proposal and, claiming that Bray had put upon him 'such an Indignity, Injury and What Not,' he announced that if Bray had not been in Holy Orders he (Seymour) would have challenged him to a duel.

Bray, accustomed as he should have been by this time to the tantrums of choleric officials, appears in this particular case to have felt pardonably exasperated.

'It is well,' he wrote to a friend, 'that we have such an Asylum as the Gown, or rather it is well for some that upon that score they may so safely bounce and hector and menace a certain Order as they please, without danger of return; which, if Chevaliers as well as themselves, I believe they would be more cautious of that sort of treatment.'

Inexcusable though Seymour's violent and discourteous outburst undoubtedly was, his disinclination to accept the Bishop's proposal was understandable. Not only was he asked, as Governor, to relinquish his powers of probate and patronage contrary to the charter under which the 'Proprietorship' of Maryland was vested in Lord Baltimore,[1] who had sole right to create courts and appoint judges; the proposal also sought to override the arrangements made by the Crown placing probate and patronage in the hands of the Governor. Furthermore, as these rights carried with them considerable emoluments, the proposals put forward by Bray and the Bishop were directed not only against the Governor's dignity but also against his bank balance. Little wonder that he was resentful.

Bray accordingly had to content himself with a letter to Major Dent, the Attorney-General of Maryland, informing him of a new commissary and requesting him to bring the matter before the Speaker of the Maryland Assembly, one Thomas Smithson, 'Out of the earnest zeal wherewith Almighty God

[1]Up to 1692, when the 'Proprietorship' and its prerogatives passed under Government control.

knows my heart still burns for the good of the Province, I would heartily wish you would renew that law whereby you formerly settled the full Ecclesiastical Jurisdiction upon the Bishop of London's Commissary.'

In 1706 Bray was once more offered the living of St Botolph Without, Aldgate, which he had declined in 1696 when he was waiting to visit Maryland. This time he accepted the benefice, which he was to occupy almost until his death in 1730. He retained his active membership of the two great Societies— S.P.C.K. and S.P.G.—in the founding of which he had played so prominent a part, but his work on their behalf in no way prevented him from performing, with characteristic energy and devotion, the work of a parish priest. For twenty-four years he was to labour in East London, at the same time continuing his efforts on behalf of negro slaves in the American colonies and in the promotion of parochial libraries.

During this period also he continued to occupy himself with his pen, publishing several books and pamphlets of a religious and missionary nature, among them his *Martyrology, or History of the Papal Aggression*, an anti-Roman treatise which he intended as a kind of supplement to Foxe's *Book of Martyrs*. His *Directorium Missionarium* was published in 1726; followed in the next year by *Primordia Bibliothecaria*, a scheme for the extension and development of his libraries project, including 'a method to proceed by a gradual Progression from Strength to Strength, from a collection not much exceeding in value one Pound to an hundred Pounds.' In 1728 Dr Bray brought out a revised *Life of Bernard Gilpin*, a sixteenth-century parish priest of saintly character and outspoken habits, popularly known as 'the Apostle of the North'. This was followed in 1729 by *A Brief Account of the Life of Mr John Rawlet*, another cleric (1642–86) who was the author of several religious works highly esteemed in their day.

*   *   *

In 1723 Bray was attacked by a dangerous illness and feeling his life to be in danger he nominated Lord Percival, Robert Hales, the Reverend Stephen Hales and William Belitha, to carry out the benefaction on behalf of the West Indian Negro slaves left by the Sieur D'Allone and to succeed Bray as trustees in the event of the latter's death. These became known as 'Dr Bray's Associates for Founding Clerical Libraries and Supporting Negro Schools'. A decree of Chancery confirmed their authority soon after Bray's death, and the Associates still fulfil the purpose for which they were called into being and a report of their activities is published annually.

Recovering from the illness, Bray continued to perform his parochial duties with exemplary zeal and later in the same year (1723) Ralph Thoresby records in his diary that he 'walked to the pious and charitable Dr Bray's in Aldgate and was extremely pleased with his many pious, useful and charitable works'. A week later he 'heard the charity children catechized in Dr Bray's Church' and remarked 'the prodigious pains so aged (Bray was 65!) a man takes'. 'He is', adds Thoresby, 'very mortified (i.e. self-disciplined) to the world, and takes abundant trouble to have a new church[1] though he would lose £100 per annum'. In 1727 Bray turned his philanthropic attention to a new field when a friend who had made a casual visit to White-chapel Prison reported to him the miserable state of the un-happy prisoners, many of whom were gaoled for debt. This account had such an effect on the Doctor that, anticipating the more thorough-going and larger-scaled efforts of John Howard by some fifty years and those of Elizabeth Fry by nearly a hundred, he at once applied himself to the task of influencing public opinion and raising funds to alleviate the wretchedness of the inmates of England's prisons. He prevailed upon many of his friends and other well-disposed persons to contribute the cost of 'Bread, Beef and Broth', on Sundays and occasional weekdays, for the prisoners in Whitechapel and Borough Compton gaols. He induced intending missionaries to visit the prisons, which in those days had no chaplains, to read and offer spiritual ministrations to the prisoners.[2]

[1]Presumably a chapel-of-ease to his existing parish church.
[2]He had much earlier taken a keen interest in the Bridewell and Newgate prisons, and in 1698 he had produced a proposal for a 'Penitentiary for Lewd Women,' a draft of which is among the papers bequeathed by Bray to Sion College.

This humanitarian work brought Bray into personal contact with the benevolent James Edward Oglethorpe, Member of Parliament for Haslemere, who early in 1729 brought the whole question of the state of the prisons before the House of Commons and succeeded in getting a Committee of Inquiry appointed, with himself as chairman. As a result of his collaboration with Bray on this question, Oglethorpe became one of the 'Associates' and persuaded other influential persons to do likewise. According to Thomas Coram, the ex-sea-captain founder of Georgia, it was Bray who suggested to Oglethorpe and others that a new colony should be founded in America for debtors and the necessitous poor who could not find employment at home—a project which Bray conceived as a kind of sequel to his two other great plans—the founding of libraries and the instruction of negroes. Shortly after Bray's death the matter was taken up by some of the Associates at a meeting on 5 March 1730, at which Oglethorpe proposed that they should apply for part of a legacy left by a Mr Joseph King wherewith to establish 'a charitable Colony for the better Maintenance of the Poor of the City of London'. The meeting adopted this scheme and on 30 July they petitioned King George II for a grant of land south of Carolina. After a delay of several months the request was granted and a royal charter issued establishing the colony and naming it Georgia in honour of His Hanoverian Majesty. Most of the Trustees named in the charter were members of Dr Bray's Associates, but as trustees of the new colony they quickly entered an independent existence of their own without connexion with the parent body, except inasmuch as they both shared the same office and secretary and in so far as several individuals continued to be members of both of these movements which drew their original inspiration from Thomas Bray.

*   *   *

In January 1730 Dr Bray became seriously ill, worn out, no doubt, in no small degree by his manifold and unending activities. As he grew progressively weaker it became imperative for some legally-constituted body to be brought into being to succeed him and his original Associates in their religious and humanitarian work. Accordingly, on 15 January a deed of appointment was drawn up constituting the Associates as a body corporate—a measure which was legally recognized and confirmed in the following year by decree of Chancery.

This was Thomas Bray's last official act and precisely one month later—on 15 February—he entered into the rest he had so richly earned.

He was buried in the church of St Botolph, Aldgate, which had been the scene of his pastoral labours for the last twenty-four years of his life. Here his name is inscribed amongst those of the other incumbents of the parish on one of the columns supporting the ceiling of the church. In 1901, to commemorate the bi-centenary of the founding of S.P.G. a tablet was placed in the church of St Michael, Chirbury, Shropshire, where Bray was baptized. The inscription on the tablet is as follows:

In Memory of
The Reverend Thomas Bray D.D.
Born at Marton in Chirbury
Baptized in this church 2nd May, 1658
Principal Founder of
The Society For Promoting Christian Knowledge
In 1698. And of
The Society for the Propagation of the Gospel
In 1701.

This Tablet was Erected In the Bi-Centenary of the Latter Society.
January 1901.

CHAPTER IV

BEHOLD, A GREAT PRIEST

ONE of the most remarkable episcopates in the history of the English Church—remarkable for its length as well as for its record of pastoral fidelity—came to an end on the 7 March in the year 1755. Thomas Wilson, forty-ninth Bishop of Sodor and Man, was 92 years of age when he died and he had been a bishop for fifty-seven of them. There may have been longer episcopates; there can have been few more distinguished ones.

Wilson, the sixth of seven children and the fifth son of middle-class parents, was born at Burton in Cheshire on the 20 December 1663. He was the nephew of Richard Sherlock, rector of Winwick in Lancashire, one of the most exemplary and respected of the later Caroline parochial clergy. This relationship is not without significance in the light of his nephew's subsequent career.

The young Thomas received his early education at the King's School, Chester, and from there proceeded, as his uncle had done, to Trinity College, Dublin, which he entered as a Sizar at the end of May, 1682. In the previous month the college had opened its doors to another youth who was as far to outshine Wilson in fame as he was to prove his inferior in spirituality—no less a person than Jonathan Swift. What kind of impact, one cannot forbear to ponder, did the future bishop make upon the future dean—if, indeed, their paths crossed at all?

At all events, it was not Gulliver's creator whose powerful personality influenced the youthful Wilson to the extent of diverting him from his chosen profession to an entirely different one. This was brought about by another of his fellow students, one Michael Hewetson,[1] who spoke to Wilson so earnestly and so persuasively of the priestly calling that in the end he abandoned his plans for pursuing a medical career and instead began to prepare himself for the reception of Holy Orders. Having taken his Bachelor of Arts degree in February 1686, he was admitted to the diaconate by William Moreton, Bishop of Kildare, on St Peter's day in that same year while still six months short of the canonical age. What form his theological studies may have taken can only be conjectured. Butler's *Analogy* and Paley's *Evidences* were still unwritten, but doubtless the College library possessed copies of the works of Hooker, Jeremy Taylor, Cosin, Pearson, Thorndike, Bramhall, and other of the great Caroline divines. We know that when he became a bishop he made much use of Cosin's *Devotions*, and doubtless that great Churchman's other writings were not unknown to him.

Although he had received his university training and his Deacon's Orders in Ireland, it was in England that Wilson sought his first curacy—in Richard Sherlock's parish of Winwick, where he was placed in charge of the outlying chapelry of Newchurch Kenyon—later to become a separate parish. Here, under his uncle's guidance, he learnt the liturgical and pastoral craftsmanship pertaining to his calling; here he laid the foundations of the spiritual eminence which was later to lift him so far above the majority of his Anglican contemporaries.

*   *   *

Wilson was ordained priest by Nicholas Stratford, Bishop of Chester, on 20 October 1689, and three years later he was appointed domestic chaplain to William George Richard Stanley, ninth Earl of Derby, and tutor to his only son James, Lord Strange. Having served his parochial novitiate, he was now to receive an invaluable introduction to the world of affairs, mixing frequently with men of rank and influence. His stipend was beggarly—a mere £30 a year—but no doubt his expenses were few, and his tastes we know were simple to the point of

[1]Later Archdeacon of Armagh, and the friend of Dr Bray.

austerity. To the end of his life, for instance, he fastened his shoes with leather thongs in place of the silver buckles normally worn by the clergy, and indeed by all with even the slightest pretension to gentility.

In the early part of 1693 his income was augmented by a further £20 a year when he was appointed to the mastership of the almshouses at Lathom. Thus raised to what must have seemed to him a state of comparative affluence, he took a solemn vow at Easter in that year to set apart one-fifth of his total income for pious purposes and for the relief of the poor. The moneys thus saved he designated his 'poor drawer', and, as time went on and his circumstances changed, the proportion of his income which went into it increased from one-fifth to a third, and then from a third to half. Apostolic poverty was no meaningless phrase when it was applied to Thomas Wilson.

Those were the days of sinecures and pluralities, and in June of 1693 Wilson's patron, Lord Derby, tried hard to persuade him to accept, in addition to his existing appointment, the valuable living of Badsworth in the West Riding of Yorkshire. But he was not of the stuff of which pluralists were made, and he firmly declined the offer. At the very outset of his ministry he had made a resolution that he would accept no preferment which would lead to his becoming a non-resident incumbent.

But for the fact that he had entered the service of the House of Stanley, Wilson might well have passed the rest of his long ministerial career in the comparative obscurity of a succession of country parishes. He was a lover of rural life, and in an age when, even more than at present, ecclesiastical preferment depended upon knowing the right people and pulling the right strings, it is doubtful whether he would have risen any higher. He would certainly have made no efforts of his own to do so.

But the Earls of Derby were also Lords of Man, the seat of an ancient Bishopric to which they had the right of appointment. The see had been vacant since the death of Bishop Baptist Levinz in 1693, possibly because it could only command an income of £300 a year. Lord Derby, in 1697, offered the appointment to his chaplain, whose austerity of life, personal integrity and moral courage he had had ample opportunities of observing at close range over the past five years. Wilson proved most unwilling to accept a bishopric, and it was only after several months and repeated urgings on the part of his patron that he finally allowed himself to be persuaded into acceptance. From what we know of Wilson's character we can well believe that the poverty of the see of Sodor and Man was as much an inducement to him to accept as it had been the cause of others declining it.

Wilson was consecrated at the Savoy Church in London on 16 January 1698, by Archbishop Sharp of York, who was assisted by Wilson's own diocesan, Bishop Stratford of Chester (who had ordained him priest) and by Bishop Moore of Norwich. To augment the scanty income of the see, Lord Derby again pressed upon him the rectory of Badsworth—to be held *in commendam*—but again the offer was declined.

That Wilson was not unmindful of the financial needs of his diocese, however, is made plain by what may be regarded as his first piece of episcopal activity. In 1675 King Charles II had granted to the diocese of Sodor and Man an annuity of £100 a year, chargeable upon the excise of beer, ale and other liquors. Wilson discovered that this annuity had not been paid for several years (possibly owing to the 'widowhood' of the see), and before leaving London he successfully applied for the payment of the arrears.

The newly-consecrated bishop landed in his island diocese, at Derby Haven, on 6 April 1698. Except for a few brief visits to Cheshire and London he was not to leave it until the day of his death fifty-seven years later. On the 11 April he was enthroned in the ruined cathedral of St German's, Peel, and took up his residence at Bishop's Court, Kirk Michael, which he found to be likewise in a ruinous condition. He immediately set about rebuilding the greater part of the derelict 'Palace' at a cost of £1,400, and it is characteristic that all but £200 of this amount came from his own private purse.

He then turned his attention to the grounds of his episcopal residence. These he found as bare and neglected as the house had proved dilapidated. With admirable energy and a prophetic foresight that might almost have envisaged what was to to be an episcopate of several decades, he proceeded to plant shrubs and trees with a view to converting the bare slopes of his ground into richly-wooded glens. Wilson's rural enthusiasms found expression, not only on his own estate, but were devoted with equal energy to fostering the agricultural resources of the island, and encouraging the farmers to adopt new methods of cultivation, cropping and irrigation. Discovering that there was no qualified physician on the island Wilson brushed up his discarded pharmaceutical learning and opened a chemist's shop, from which he dispensed simple drugs and remedies and attended as best he could to the physical ailments of his flock. His early medical training had not been entirely a waste of time. Later, a qualified doctor arrived on the island and Wilson at once handed over to him his 'practice' and supplies of drugs. The new physician's name was Thomas Cruttwell. He became a warm admirer of Wilson and eventually, under the Bishop's influence, he too relinquished the pursuit of medicine and was admitted to Holy Orders. After Wilson's death, Cruttwell wrote the first biography of him, which work was published in 1781.

To the 'poor drawer' in his desk Wilson soon added a 'poor chest' in his barn, always kept well-filled with corn for supplying the needy who might otherwise have gone without their daily bread. He furthermore had always on hand an ample stock of assorted pairs of spectacles so that the indigent aged, as their eyesight began to fail them, might still be able to read their Bibles and Prayer Books and also, as he put it, 'use their glasses to help them thread a needle and mend their cloaks'. Under Bishop Wilson's fatherly care, the wants of the under-privileged Manxman were quietly attended to by the Welfare Church 200 years before the politicians and social scientists announced with mighty trumpetings the advent of the Welfare State.

The long-neglected diocese of Sodor and Man provided ample scope for its new bishop's ebullient spirits, and he enthusiastically applied himself to the tasks which he found awaiting him. The erection of new churches was one of the matters in which he quickly began to occupy himself—to replace older buildings which had become either ruinous be-

yond repair, or too small for the needs of an increasing population. A further scheme which claimed his interest was that
launched around the turn of the century, by Dr Thomas Bray,
for the establishing of parochial libraries, both in England and
in the American colonies. Wilson wholeheartedly supported
this undertaking, and took the initiative in setting up several
such libraries throughout the Island of Man. In his posthumously published *Sacra Privata*, against the year 1699, appears
this entry: 'By ye encouragement and assistance of my worthy
Freind (*sic*) Dr. Tho. Bray, I began this year a Foundation of
Parochial Librarys in this Diocese; which by the Good Blessing
of God upon His servant, I have been improving ever since with
Books both Practical and Devotional.' Wilson's name, incidentally, appears on a list of 'Correspondents' of the newly-
launched Society for Promoting Christian Knowledge, dated
31 October 1699. It was probably his interest and activity in this
work of founding parochial libraries which led the Bishop to
appreciate the urgent need for books written in the ancient Manx
language—at that time still widely known and spoken throughout the island. Having set himself the task of learning and master-
ing Manx, he wrote and in 1707 published his *Principles and
Duties of Christianity—in English and Manks, with short and plain
Directions and Prayers*. This, the first book ever to be published in
Manx, is frequently referred to as *The Manx Catechism*, and was
followed by *A Further Instruction*. In 1733 Wilson produced a
devotional and doctrinal treatise on the Eucharist entitled,
A Short and Plain Instruction for the Lord's Supper. Fairly early
in his episcopate he set himself the task of translating the
Bible into Manx, an undertaking which, in spite of the surpassing vitality and length of years vouchsafed to him, he
found beyond his powers to complete. St Matthew's Gospel
in Manx appeared in 1722, but although the other Gospels and
the Acts of the Apostles were translated under Wilson's supervision, they were not, in fact, published during his lifetime.

Unhampered by the Act of Uniformity, which was not
applicable to the Isle of Man, Wilson found himself free to
supplement the Liturgy of the Book of Common Prayer with
prayers and services which he compiled to meet particular

needs and to provide for special occasions. Although a supporter of the Revolution settlement, he was a convinced High Churchman and from the outset of his episcopate set out to banish what he regarded as the bad custom of having celebrations of the Holy Communion only two or three times a year. Yet, in spite of the firmness with which he held to his own convictions, there was nothing of the fanatic or bigot about him. Roman Catholics delighted to attend his services, and so did dissenters of Protestant persuasion. Wilson won the hearts of the latter by respecting what he knew to be one of their most cherished foibles. It had long been a point of Puritan principle to decline to kneel at Communion. Wilson let it be known that whenever they cared to be present at the Anglican Liturgy they were free to sit or stand as they felt inclined. As a consequence, not being *compelled* to kneel, they freely elected to do so. There may be some sort of a moral here for modern efforts in the cause of reunion. While, admittedly, more vital matters divide us, might it not be that greater flexibility on the part of Anglicans with regard to posture during divine service would help to dissipate a good deal of distaste for our ways of worship on the part of those who are used to more free and easy methods? Is it absolutely essential that every servant of the Lord should be found in precisely the same posture at a given moment of the service? They order these things differently, and certainly less rigidly, in Roman and Eastern Orthodox churches, where the faithful are free to stand, sit or kneel as their devotion moves them, and no censorious glances are cast at any who elect to adopt a position different from that taken up by the majority present. So long as reverence is observed and the convenience and susceptibilities of others respected, surely it cannot matter greatly whether one sits, stands or kneels—although Anglicans will probably always feel that it is more seemly to stand for the singing of psalms and hymns, as well as for the recitation of the Creed, and to kneel for prayers and blessings and to receive the Body and Blood of their Lord in Holy Communion.

Characteristic of Wilson's high sacramental outlook and conviction was the extreme conscientiousness with which he discharged his solemn duty of preparing and ordaining candidates for the sacred ministry. Firmly persuaded that the character of a Church depended in no small degree upon the character of the clergy who served it, he exercised a discretion in the choice of candidates for Orders which was utterly untypical of contemporary episcopal practice. Whereas most of his fellow-bishops required little in the way of pastoral training or proof of vocation and were prepared to lay hands suddenly on anyone with sufficient social or political pull, Wilson had very different views. From the very beginning of his episcopate he had revived the ancient custom of consulting annually with his clergy in Synod—a proceeding far removed from the present-day Diocesan Conference, which is inevitably occupied mainly with material problems, and where policy is invariably decided upon beforehand and, announced from the platform, requires little more than the rubber stamp of a general approval. At these annual Synods or Convocations, happily free from State control or interference of any kind, he would discuss with his clergy the men whose names were before him as seeking ordination. In a small diocese and on a sparsely populated island, it was no doubt possible for most of them to be known to one or more of the parochial clergy, who were asked to approve each individual candidate, knowing that only those receiving such approbation would be permitted to go forward to ordination. The approval duly given—or withheld—the members of Synod were asked to exercise a watchful care over the accepted men so that they could, in due course, sign their testimonials from personal knowledge and with a clear conscience.

The successful candidates were then taken to reside for a whole year in the Bishop's own household, which in this way fulfilled the function of a theological college, Wilson himself reading the Greek Testament with his students every day. Then, as now, there was a serious shortage of candidates for the Ministry, and to meet the immediate needs of his diocese he was compelled to seek sanction from the Archbishop of York for the ordination of certain men below the canonical ages of 23 for deacons and 24 for priests. It will be remembered that Wilson himself had been ordained deacon by Bishop Moreton of Kildare while still six months short of the requisite age. One of the earliest of those to be ordained by Wilson was a certain William Walker who ultimately became one of the Bishop's most trusted friends and fellow-workers. At the age of thirteen Walker was employed in the capacity of general handy lad by a Mr Stevenson of Ballydoole. One day, driving his master's cart home from the harvest field, he allowed himself to become absorbed in a book. The horse, finding the reins hanging loose upon his neck, wandered amiably across the front lawn of the house and came to a halt before the parlour window where Mr Stevenson was standing. Rushing from the house he confronted the embarrassed William.

'Since thou art so fond of reading,' he announced, 'thou shalt have thy fill of it.' And the very next day the boy was packed off to Castletown Academy, where by diligence and good conduct he profited admirably by this turn of fortune and made rapid progress in his studies. He was ordained deacon in March 1700, and priest on Trinity Sunday, 31 May 1702.

Wilson was married at Winwick, on 27 October 1698, to Mary Patten by whom he had four children. Only one of them, his son Thomas, survived him. Thomas, born at Bishop's Court on 24 August 1703, was ordained and for a short time assisted his father on the island. He is said to have left at the end of this period on account of his inability to master the Manx tongue. He became successively a Royal Chaplain; rector of St Stephen's, Wallbrook, rector of St Margaret's and prebendary of Westminster, dying at Bath on 15 April 1784.

Bishop Wilson's married life was a short one, for his wife died on 7 March 1705. A few months after his marriage he had firmly resolved that he would:

(1) more diligently follow my studies;
(2) immediately regulate my devotions and attend to them constantly;
(3) preach more constantly;
(4) compose prayers for the poor families, in order to have them printed;
(5) endeavour with all my might to withdraw my heart from the care of the things of this world.

These resolutions, diligently persevered in, provided the

keynote of his public and private behaviour throughout the long
years of his active ministry.

'During the fifty-eight years of pastoral (i.e. episcopal) life',
writes his first biographer, Thomas Cruttwell, 'except on
occasions of sickness, he never failed on a Sunday to expound the
Scripture, to preach the Gospel, or administer the Sacrament,
at some one or other of the churches of his diocese; and if absent
from the island, he always preached at the church where he
resided for the day.'

Yet another of his biographers, Hugh Stowell, gives us an
appealing glimpse of the Bishop beneath his own roof.

The Bishop was regular and devout in the observance of
family worship. The whole family constantly assembled in his
chapel at six o'clock every morning during the summer season,
and at seven in the winter, when he himself, or one of the candidates for the holy ministry who were inmates of his house, offered
up solemn prayer. The evening sacrifice was performed in the
same manner at a stated hour.

As he arranged all his affairs with exact method, so he conducted his family devotions with particular order and regularity.
At the appointed hour of prayer, a servant entered the room
where the Bishop was sitting, and with a respectful bow, uttered
these words: 'My Lord, all things are ready'. Instantly the Bishop
arose and with holy joy applied himself to his favourite work.
Whoever were his guests, or whatever was his employment, the
morning and evening sacrifice was never intermitted.

It is related that on one occasion, when he had a large company at his house consisting of foreigners and persons of different
religious persuasions, the servant entered the parlour at the
hallowed hour with the usual intonation. His Lordship having
apologised to the company for leaving them, telling them that he
was going to pray with his people, immediately retired; but no
sooner had he reached the chapel than every one of his guests
followed, as if constrained by an involuntary impulse and an
irresistible attraction.

Perhaps under the influence of Dr Bray's stimulating example, Wilson founded a public library at Castletown in 1702,
and by the help of generous benefactions from various sources

—notably from Lady Elizabeth Hastings—he successfully strove to increase the number and efficiency of grammar and parochial schools on the island. Nor were his interests purely insular, for in 1724 he founded, and later endowed, a grammar school at Burton, his Cheshire birthplace. After the parish churches themselves, the schools of his diocese were always his closest concern, and he laid perpetual stress upon the necessity for the clergy to visit and teach in them. This they were urged to regard as a solemn and indispensable duty—a theme to which he returned again and again in his visitation charges and pastoral letters. Perhaps it was in recognition of these educational endeavours that the University of Oxford, in May 1707, bestowed upon him the degree of Doctor of Divinity.

But perhaps the task for which Bishop Wilson's episcopate is most famous, which from its very outset engaged his most strenuous efforts, and which brought him determined opposition from a dissident minority, was that of restoring that ancient discipline of the Primitive Church which the Prayer Book, in its introductory rubrics to the Commination Service, refers to as a thing greatly to be desired. Wilson's views on this question are forcibly expounded in his *Sacra Privata*.

> 'Church discipline,' he said, 'is for the honour of God, for the safety of religion, the good of sinners, and for the public weal, that sinners may not run headlong into ruin without being made sensible of their danger; that others may see and fear and not go on presumptuously in their evil ways; that the house of God may not become a den of thieves; and that judgments may not be poured down on the whole community. The most effectual way of answering these ends is to exercise a strict, impartial discipline. First, to withhold from offenders the benefit of the Holy Sacrament, till they behave themselves so as to be worthy of so great a blessing; and secondly, if they continue obstinate (all proper methods being used to reclaim them), to excommunicate them, and to oblige all sober Christians not to have familiar converse with them.'

All this, of course, is profoundly shocking to what is by courtesy known as the modern mind. That a political party, a trades union, the boy scout movement, the fighting services, the medical and legal professions, commercial undertakings and a thousand and one voluntary organizations of every conceivable kind should have, and exercise, the right to discipline their erring members is considered to be so unquestionably axiomatic as almost to constitute one of the natural laws of the universe. None but the erring are normally disposed to challenge it. But let the Church presume to exercise such a right in the case of her adherents, let her essay to apply to her Master's admonition that all who refuse to hear her remonstrances should be to the faithful as the heathen and the publican, and immediately indignant voices are uplifted, denunciatory pens are dipped in gall, and from all sides come volleys of abuse and accusations of bigotry, uncharity and obscurantism. Such illogical and unfair sentimentalism passes muster easily enough in an age which so frequently seeks to reduce religion to a very elastic morality tinged with a particularly nauseating brand of emotionalism; it would have been repudiated as humbug and cant by the clear-thinking realism of the early eighteenth century. For the Church to turn a blind eye to notorious evil livers in her own ranks, to admit such malefactors to her most sacred ministrations, was to be guilty of gross dereliction of a plainly obvious duty. 'Whom the Lord loveth He chasteneth', and for the Church to fail to penalize the blatant and impenitent wrongdoer was to fail in fatherly correction and love.

Neither was there here any question of denominational particularity. The Roman Catholic Church through the confessional, the Presbyterians through the Kirk Session, the early Methodists by means of the penitents' bench, all exercised such discipline with greater or more systematic severity than was commonly the practice in Anglican parishes. The Church of England was already imperceptibly slipping towards that latitudinarian laxity which has come to full growth in present-day indifference to Christian principles and ecclesiastical authority on the part of so many nominal Church members. Only in his comparatively remote island diocese, far out in the Irish Sea, was there still a bishop who ruled his flock as a strict but loving father, one who refused to court easy popularity by pretending that sins were something else, who would not contribute to the ruination of souls by withholding the salutary voice of warning and rebuke, and, if that should fail, was ready to impose, however reluctantly, the sanctions and penalties prescribed by ecclesiastical law.

These ancient 'spiritual statutes' of the island still legally valid where they had not been specifically superseded by the Canons of 1603, were of local growth and by the time of Wilson's arrival generally inadequate. Without attempting to have them repealed or discredited,[1] he proceeded to draw up his own 'Ecclesiastical Constitutions'. These, ten in all, were subscribed to by the clergy of the diocese in Synod, at Bishop's Court, on 3 February 1704; ratified by the Governor and Council of the island, confirmed by the Earl of Derby[2] and proclaimed on Tynwald Hill on 6 June in the same year. It was of these Constitutions that a future Lord Chancellor, Sir Peter King, remarked, 'If the ancient discipline of the Church were lost, it might be found in all its purity in the Isle of Man.'

A word should perhaps be said here about the peculiar status of the Church Courts in the Isle of Man, where the pre-Reformation Chapter Courts—long since discontinued in England and Wales—still survived. These were held half-yearly, one or both of the Vicars-General (sometimes, in Kirk Michael at least, the Bishop himself) sitting to receive presentments from local clergy and churchwardens. The proceedings were always *viva voce*. The Consistory, or Bishop's Courts, heard appeals from the Chapter Courts, granted probate of all wills, and dealt with the more serious disciplinary matters as well as with certain 'reserved cases'. Here the proceedings were chiefly documentary. Both Courts were held competent to deal with *lay offenders*, as well as clerical ones, against the moral and ecclesiastical laws.

A point which had once been hotly disputed was whether the Final Court of Appeal should be the Archbishop of York, as Metropolitan, or the Governor and Council, as representing the secular power. This was ultimately decided in favour of the

---

[1]Except that which permitted public penance to be commuted by payment of a fine.

[2]The tenth Earl, Wilson's former pupil.

Archbishop, by James, the 'Great' Earl of Derby, in 1636, when an ordinance was passed by him, as Lord of the Island, forbidding appeals from ecclesiastical courts

> to the Lieutenant, or to the Captain, or to his Deputie, or to the Judges, or 24 Keys or any of them, for any cause depending or determined in the Ecclesiastical Courts, which do merely concern Government of the Church, Excommunications, Suspensions, Incests, Adultery, Fornication, Profanation of the Sabbath, Cursing, Probate of Wills and Testaments, Granting of (Letters of) Administration, granting Tuition of Infants' goods, or merely subtracting of Tythes, or for or concerning the Defamations determinable or punishable by Ecclesiastical Laws.

The Episcopal officials whose duty it was to administer this discipline through the ecclesiastical courts of the island were: the Archdeacon and his Official; two Vicars General; the Diocesan and Archidiaconal Registrars; and the Sumner, or Summoner-General, who had a deputy in each parish and whose function it was to deliver citations and serve judgements of the courts on the parties concerned. The Archdeacon was nominated, rather oddly, by the Lord of the Island; the Vicars-General by the Bishop, as were also the Registrars and Sumner.

This was, then, the disciplinary system which Wilson found in at any rate theoretical existence on his arrival in the island, and which he felt himself morally obliged to revive, restore and administer—a system, it will readily be observed, which, though clearly envisaged in the Canons of 1604, and though still capable of being put into efficient operation in the Isle of Man, had long ceased to be anything but a shadow elsewhere in the Church of England. It was, furthermore, a system which, however much it may in some respects have erred in over-severity, was at least a wholesome contrast to the lack of system, the moral anarchy and indifference, which generally prevailed on the mainland. It was largely for want of such a system throughout her communion as a whole that the Church of England steadily lost, during the next 200 years, the position of authority in the country which was rightfully hers as Defender of the Faith and upholder of Christian morals.

The 'Constitutions' covered a wide variety of offences and applied impartially to clergy and laity alike. When sentence had been passed by the ecclesiastical court the civil authorities were required to give it effect without delay or modification. These sentences were certainly not empty formalities. A certain John Robinson, who had slandered a Deemster by calling him a church robber, was ordered to be

> immediately committed to St. German's prison, there to continue till he give in sufficient security to do three Sunday's penance, after a very solemn and humble manner, viz, one in Kirk Arbory, one in Kirk Christ Rushen, and one in Kirk Malew, and in each church humbly ask forgiveness of the said Deemster Parr, and lay his finger on his mouth, saying, 'Tongue thou hast lied,' and all along so demean himself as becomes a true penitent, and to behave himself for the future respectfully towards the said Deemster.

Another offender, one John Kneale, was required to present himself on nine consecutive Sundays at nine different churches and to ask the incumbent, as he went into morning service, for permission to 'satisfy your congregation that I am heartily grieved for my great offences against God and man; that I purpose by the grace of God to become a new man. To which end I desire your and their pardon and prayers'. He was then to wait near the church door till the service was ended, when he was to receive from the parish priest a certificate to the effect that he had 'strictly examined him before the people touching the truth and sincerity of his repentance'.

Penalties such as these, however hurtful they may have been to personal pride, involved no physical suffering on the part of those who incurred them. At least one sentence, however, appals us by its almost savage severity, and must unfortunately be regarded as a most regrettable and inexcusable lapse from the compassion and human sympathy which Wilson normally showed and which so endeared him to all who knew him. Here, for once, the quality of mercy is not merely strained but seemingly entirely absent. This was the case of a notorious prostitute, Kath Kinred of Kirk Christ, who, all warnings and admonitions having failed to reform her, was sentenced to be dragged behind a boat in the sea in March . . . 'To which end, a boat and boat's crew are to be charged by the General Sumner, and the constables and soldiers of the garrison are to be aiding and assisting in seeing this censure performed'.

This lamentable sentence was signed, on 15 March 1713, both by Wilson and by William Walker, whom he had recently appointed as one of the Vicars-General. It constitutes the one serious blot upon the otherwise blameless record of Wilson's long and magnificent episcopate. All that can be said by way of extenuation is that his abhorrence of the woman's openly-flaunted and long-persisted-in immorality betrayed him into a severity far beyond the deserts of the offence in question, a severity quite foreign to his stern but normally just and compassionate nature. As it happened, the sea was too rough on the day appointed (St Patrick's Day—17 March) for the execution of the sentence, and it was carried out some days later instead. Nor was it sufficient to reform the hapless Kate who relapsed into her old ways, was again tried and sentenced to the same punishment, with twenty-one days' imprisonment and a public penance to be performed in all churches of the island in addition. This time the discipline appears to have been effective, and after a period of probation the Bishop ordered her to be received back into the full communion and fellowship of the Church.

During this same year of 1713 came the first serious conflict between the spiritual and the secular powers in the island. Robert Mawdesley, Governor from 1703, had worked in close and invariable harmony with the Bishop. In 1713 he left the island and was succeeded as Governor by Alexander Horne, who from the outset became Wilson's determined opponent. At first his opposition consisted mainly of minor pinpricks and general unwillingness to co-operate. But in 1716 came a direct clash. Mary Henricks, a married woman, was excommunicated for adultery, and condemned to penance and prison. She appealed to the Governor and Horne allowed her appeal. Wilson, maintaining that an appeal lay only to the Archbishop of York, as Metropolitan, refused to attend its hearing, and was consequently fined £10. This fine was subsequently remitted, but some time later the Episcopal Registrar, John Woods, was imprisoned by the Governor by refusing to act in this case without direction from the Bishop.

The next conflict between Wilson and Horne, in 1721, led to more serious consequences. It involved no less a person than the Governor's wife, who was ordered to ask forgiveness (in mitigation of penance) for making slanderous statements. When she refused to do so, the Governor's chaplain, Archdeacon Robert Horrobin, admitted her to communion. Wilson, who had already had occasion to deplore on Horrobin's part certain heretical tendencies, promptly suspended him. Horne equally promptly demanded that this suspension be withdrawn. Wilson refused to withdraw it, and was fined £50. When he declined to pay this fine, he and his Vicars-General (who had each been fined £20) were imprisoned in Rushen Castle. This was on 29 June.

It is a remarkable tribute to the tremendous esteem in which Wilson was held that, in spite of the unpalatable nature of many of his disciplinary measures, public sympathy in the island was entirely on his side. Every day large crowds gathered outside the prison demanding the Bishop's release and imploring his blessing. The window of his cell looked out on the square where the people gathered and through its bars he preached to them, exhorting them to peaceful behaviour and faithful Church membership. But for his influence with them, they would have attacked the Governor's house and possibly the Governor himself.

Wilson, from his prison, appealed to the Crown and on 31 August came an order for his release. The fines of the Bishop and the Vicars-General were paid by one Thomas Corlett. He had only been in prison for two months, but the dampness of his cell so affected Wilson's fingers that henceforth he was unable to move them for the purpose of writing and was forced to hold the pen in his fist. He used to claim humorously that his diocese was never better governed than when he was in prison, but this unfortunate experience left its mark upon his health for the rest of his life.

In 1724 he was actually offered the Bishopric of Exeter by

way of compensation for what he had suffered, but he declined to accept it, just as he had previously begged leave to refuse another bishopric of far greater wealth than his own which he was offered by Queen Anne. This offer was made on one of Wilson's rare visits to London,[1] when he was commanded to preach before the Queen. She was so delighted by the eloquence of the Bishop's sermon, as well as by what she had heard of his character and pastoral zeal, that she thought to honour him by the proffered advancement. His refusal was characteristic. He explained that he felt that by the blessing of God he could do some little good in the little spot that he then resided on; whereas if he were removed to a larger sphere, he might be lost and forget his duty to his flock and to his God.

Wilson's doctrinal dispute with Horrobin had arisen over the latter's approval of a book that the Bishop had already censured as irreligious—a book entitled *The Independent Whig*, published in 1721. This work was made use of by Governor Horne and his Archdeacon in the prosecution of their vendetta against the Bishop. A copy of the book had been sent to Wilson by a layman, John Stevenson, who in turn had received it from a certain Richard Worthington as a gift for the public library. On 27 January 1722, Wilson issued a pastoral letter condemning the work and instructing the clergy to excommunicate all 'agents and abettors' of it 'and such-like blasphemous books'. Horne struck at Wilson through Stevenson, by imprisoning the latter in Rushen Castle and then demanding, as a condition of Stevenson's release, that Wilson hand over the book to the public library. When the book reached William Ross, the librarian, the latter said that he would as soon take poison as receive it into the library 'upon any other terms or conditions than immediately to burn it'. Whether Ross had the temerity thus to dispose of the volume in defiance of the Governor is not clear, but Horne was superseded in the following year so no doubt it was destroyed after he had departed from the island, if not before.

Floyd, Horne's successor, was generally unpopular and his period of office was a brief one. In 1725 he in turn was succeeded

[1] In 1711.

by Thomas Horton, and almost at once a fresh conflict started between the civil and ecclesiastical powers. Lord Derby now claimed that the Act of Henry VIII which placed Man in the province of York abrogated all island laws in matters spiritual. Horton consequently refused to confirm and carry out a recent decision of the Manx Parliament[1] that soldiers should be allowed to execute orders of the ecclesiastical courts. With Wilson's concurrence, the House of Keys then proposed a complete revision of the spiritual statutes. Horton immediately suspended the whole code 'till amended and revised'. He also took it upon himself to dismiss the Sumner-General and appoint another—a flagrant usurpation of a prerogative of the Bishop. Unavailing petitions for redress were sent to Lord Derby; and in November 1728 the House of Keys appealed to the King, but with the same lack of success. The deadlock was not resolved until the death of Lord Derby in 1736, when the Lordship of Man (in the absence of a male heir) passed to James Murray, second Duke of Atholl. A revision of the ecclesiastical statutes was at once proceeded with and carried through, resulting happily in a cessation of the dispute between the civil and spiritual courts. Between Wilson and the Duke of Atholl, and the Governors of the latter's appointing, relations appear to have been entirely amicable with a marked absence of the friction which had existed formerly. Under the revised code of ecclesiastical law, presentments for moral offices became markedly less frequent, although Wilson still sedulously administered discipline through the spiritual courts, especially with regard to the clergy.

On six separate occasions, over some twenty years, he found it his painful duty to pronounce sentence of suspension upon one of the clergy of his diocese—of whom there were never more than about twenty-five at any given time. One priest he was forced to suspend a second time, after reconciliation. A deacon was suspended for three years for marrying two minors without obtaining the consent of their respective parents. A priest received a similar sentence for firing off guns at night and so disturbing the peaceful and slumbering citizens of Castletown—a curious form of amusement for which its perpetrator

[1]House of Keys.

seems to have been amply penalized. Stern disciplinarian Wilson undoubtedly was, but at least his chastisements fell, with the greatest impartiality, upon cleric and layman alike.

Henceforth he ranked as a leading member of the Governor's Council, a duty which he seems to have discharged conscientiously.[1] He could never be induced, however, to sit in the House of Lords, although by courtesy there is a seat set apart for the Bishops of Man[2] detached from those of the other Bishops and within the Bar of the House. He defended his refusal by saying that the Church should have nothing to do with the State since Christ's Kingdom is not of this world—a somewhat peculiar and illogical position for one who occupied a seat on the Governor's Council and who, furthermore, had never hesitated to invoke the aid of the secular arm to give effect to the sentences and censures of the courts spiritual. It is, however, a minor blemish in one of such surpassing moral excellence as Wilson—one of those endearing foibles, perhaps, which serve to reassure the rest of sinful, toiling, aspiring mankind of the essential humanity of the very great and to dissipate the despair which might otherwise be their portion; a touch of nature to emphasize the kinship and common clay of saint and sinner alike.

In 1735 Wilson met, in London, General J. E. Oglethorpe, friend of debtors and founder of the Colony of Georgia. This meeting led to a renewed interest in overseas missionary work on Wilson's part, although he had for long been a warm supporter of both S.P.C.K. and S.P.G. At Oglethorpe's suggestion he wrote an *Essay Towards an Instruction for the Indians . . . in Dialogues*, which was published in 1740 and dedicated to the Georgia trustees. Wilson also drew up a scheme for the training of missionaries. His most famous work, *Sacra Privata*, a classic of Anglican devotional writing, was published posthumously, in 1781, as part of Cruttwell's *Life of Wilson*. The Oxford edition of 1838 carried a preface by John Henry Newman in

---

[1] A predecessor, Bishop Isaac Barrow (1663–1671), had himself held office as Governor, and was known as a 'Sword Bishop'—*i.e.* as having the Sword of State borne before him.

[2] He is not allowed to vote.

which that great master of English says of Wilson's literary style: 'There is nothing in him but what is plain, direct, homely, for the most part prosaic; all is sober, unstrained, rational, severely chastened in style and language.'

*　　*　　*

In the year 1749 Wilson was the recipient of a curious mark of distinction from outside his own country and communion. For some years he had been interested in the Moravian Brotherhood, of whose leader, Count Zinzendorf, he had heard much through mutual friends. He had also had some correspondence with Henry Cossart, author of *A Short Account of the Moravian Churches*, and now he received from Zinzendorf and his colleagues a letter accompanied by a copy of the Moravian Catechism.

No doubt the object of this was to further the cause of unity between the Moravians and the Church of England, a project stimulated in the eighteenth century by John Wesley's contacts with them. The Moravians, or *Unitas Fratrum*, are a small Evangelical sect claiming somewhat doubtfully to have preserved the historic episcopate and tracing a tenuous existence back to the fifteenth century. In Wilson's time their principal centre was at Hernhutt in Saxony, though many of their missionaries were working in England and America. They followed a strict rule of life, adopted a vegetarian diet, met daily for common devotions as well as for mutual support and edification, and practised a form of quietism which was ultimately the cause of Wesley's breaking with them.

In September 1749 Count Zinzendorf was in London, where a Synod of the English Moravian province was taking place, when news came of the death of a certain Cochius of Berlin who was one of the 'Antecessors' of the Moravian General Synod. The vacant post—a somewhat nebulous and purely honorific one, it would seem—was offered to Wilson by Zinzendorf, who sent with the offer a signet ring. Wilson accepted the office, which he retained for the rest of his life. The courtesy, pleasing one though it undoubtedly was, does not appear to have accomplished anything in the way of steps towards reunion. This was not a matter to which Anglican bishops of the Hanoverian period gave much thought or attention, and although the Lambeth Conference of 1897 expressed 'a hearty desire for such relations with (the Moravians) as will aid the cause of unity', and appointed a committee to examine the question of their Orders, the position with regard to reunion with them remains broadly what it was 200 years ago.

A contact of a different kind was that established in 1743 when Wilson received a letter from the French Cardinal Fleury, who, remarking that they must be the 'two oldest and he believed the two poorest bishops in Europe', invited Wilson to visit him in France. His Eminence was so delighted with the Anglican bishop's reply that he is credited with having obtained from Louis XV an order prohibiting French privateers from ravaging the Isle of Man.

Towards the end of his life Wilson paid one of his few visits to London, where crowds surrounded him in the streets, imploring his blessing. He was received at Court and presented to King George II, not a remarkably religious man, who, nevertheless, was moved to ask his visitor to remember him in his prayers. At a levee attended by several of the English bishops he was greeted on his entry by Queen Caroline turning to the assembled prelates with the often quoted remark, 'See, my lords, here comes a bishop who does not seek a translation!' Wilson's reply is equally historic: 'No, and it please your Majesty, I will not leave my wife in her old age because she is poor'.

So he returned to his island diocese where he devoted his remaining years to the spiritual needs of those to whose parents and grandparents he had ministered over more than half a century. From 1750, his eighty-sixth year, he was crippled with gout but no thought of retirement seems to have entered his head. Five more years of devoted labour remained to him until, on 7 March 1755, still in harness, he finally laid down the pastoral care and entered his well-won rest.

He had a strong objection to burials inside churches, and so his grave was dug at the east end of Kirk Michael churchyard. His coffin was made from an elm tree which he himself had

B.B.—G

planted soon after his arrival on the island. A few years before his death he had had it felled and sawn into planks for this very purpose.

A square marble monument marks the spot where, in characteristic simplicity, the Manx folk laid to rest from his life-long labours—like a second St John on his northern Patmos—Thomas Wilson, servant of God, patriarch, confessor and the glory of his times.

CHAPTER V

FOUNDING FATHER

NATHANIEL WOODARD, son of an Essex gentleman and ninth child in a family of twelve, was born on St Benedict's Day, 21 March, in the year 1811.

The family circumstances appear to have been somewhat straitened and Nathaniel's childhood and youth darkened by the ever-present shadow of impecuniosity—a circumstance which undoubtedly helps to account for his intense concern in later life over the difficulties experienced by what were commonly termed the lower middle-classes in making ends meet and, above all, in providing their sons with a sound education. The austerity of Woodard's early life and upbringing is exemplified by the fact that he himself was never sent to school and was consequently deprived of a systematic grounding in any of the various branches of knowledge—with one notable exception. His mother was a woman of profound piety and spiritual force, and whatever her children may have lacked of elementary secular learning their religious training was thoroughly attended to.

The young Nathaniel seems to have been conscious, from an early age, of a clear vocation to the priesthood, a conviction which no subsequent frustration or difficulty was ever able to shake. His intense seriousness of purpose appears in a document drawn up by him at the age of 19 and put away in an old tin box, where it remained undisturbed till his death, when it was accidentally brought to light. This document was headed 'My Covenant with God, which I swear to keep by His grace', and in it he pledges himself to loyal and life-long discipleship. It is perhaps a somewhat precocious and over-piously expressed effusion to come from the pen of a young man of 19, but of its sincerity there can be no doubt. Full of a spirit of penitence and a deep sense of personal unworthiness, it contains a truly humble supplication for divine help and guidance.

In a belated attempt to remedy his lack of formal schooling Woodard was sent to read with an East Anglian country clergyman, the Reverend W. Stratton, Rector of Broughton, Norfolk. His father, however, could hold out no hope of ever being able to afford to send him to Oxford or Cambridge, and as the bishops at that time invariably refused to ordain any but university men Nathaniel for a time seems to have despaired of taking Holy Orders in the Church of England and even to have contemplated entering the Nonconformist ministry.

He must have made rapid strides with his studies under Mr Stratton for in 1832 he became tutor to the family of a Mr Leicester, a man of some academic distinction who had been Senior Wrangler in the year of Waterloo. Leicester formed a high opinion of Nathaniel's mathematical ability and urged his father to send him to Cambridge. Woodard senior now felt able to agree to this, but just when it had been arranged for Nathaniel to proceed to the university some further unspecified financial difficulty intervened to render this impossible. However, just when all once more seemed utterly hopeless, another sudden reversal of fortune occurred. Through the kindness, it is believed, of two aunts, money sufficient to send him to a university was made available to Woodard and on the strength of this windfall he became engaged to a Miss Elizabeth Brill. They were married at Nettleswell in Essex on 24 March 1836.

In July 1833 John Keble had preached his famous 'Assize Sermon' which had launched the Oxford Movement upon its long and fateful course and when, in 1834, Woodard went up, not after all to Cambridge, but to Magdalen Hall, Oxford, which forty years later was to be dissolved and its fellows and students incorporated in Hertford College, the *Tracts for the Times* were stirring the Church of England from its century of torpor and self-stultification. The Church was being vehemently recalled to its true vocation and reminded of its divine commission and origin.

Woodard's time at Oxford was spent in this invigorating atmosphere of spiritual ferment and renewed vitality, and it would have been surprising indeed if one so filled with religious zeal and fervour had remained unmoved and unaffected by what was a subject of almost daily debate and violent clash of opinion. He was not unaffected for while he never permitted himself to be drawn into purely factional fights or formal party affiliations, Woodard's life-long ecclesiastical principles were irrevocably and unswervingly those to which the Oxford Fathers bore their firm and unflinching witness. The Creeds, the Apostolic Succession of the episcopate, the Sacraments of the Church, the Book of Common Prayer and its Catechism, after the bible itself, became in those formative Oxford years the sure foundations upon which were based his ecclesiastical outlook and his life's endeavours.

Woodard found himself then, and ever afterwards remained, a Catholic *sans phrase*, without prefix or qualification and undeviating in his loyalty to Anglicanism and Anglican standards; in no sense of the word was he ever a 'party' man, nor did he ever indulge in the more disruptive proclivities of ecclesiastical party politics which to so many young Churchmen, and not infrequently to their seniors, constituted a snare and diversion from matters of vaster consequence.

*　　*　　*

After his marriage Woodard found himself working under obvious difficulties and distractions so that he did not take his degree until 1840. On 6 June of the following year he was ordained deacon by Bishop Blomfield of London.

Although he was not, at first, formally licensed, he was at once thrust into a position of responsibility by being placed in sole charge of the newly-formed ecclesiastical district of St Bartholomew's, Bethnal Green—an incredible appointment to be held by an inexperienced, newly-ordained deacon who had not even had the benefit of a period of practical training at a theological college. The Bishop apparently promised Woodard that as soon as the church was consecrated and the district constuted as a separate, independent parish he should become its first vicar.

For all his want of training and experience Woodard soon proved himself an indefatigable worker and a conscientious shepherd of souls, exhibiting even at this early stage of his career that remarkable talent for raising large sums of money which later he was to put to such outstandingly successful uses. Not only did he see his church completed; he also built and equipped a school, to raise the funds for which he stood guarantor for amounts far beyond his personal capacity to find. This may be regarded either as an example of outstanding faith or of extreme foolhardiness, but of the courage and confidence which lay behind the rashness there can be no question. These were qualities in which Woodard was pre-eminent and they constitute probably the main secret of his remarkable acccomplishments.

Nathaniel Woodard was ordained priest in 1842, and with three small children to provide for he now sought from the Bishop of London the fulfilment of his promise to make the district of St Bartholomew's a separate parish with himself as its first vicar.

But at this juncture another of fate's sudden and inexplicable convolutions occurred to affect the whole course of his career and eventually to launch him upon his life-time's labours. In May 1843 he preached a sermon in St Bartholomew's on the subject of private confession and priestly absolution at which a person in the congregation took offence and complained to the Bishop. The latter asked to see the sermon, a copy of which was duly sent to him. Although Woodard had advocated nothing which went beyond what could be deduced from Holy Scripture or was authorized by the Book of Common Prayer, Blomfield took a highly unfavourable view of the sermon, stigmatizing it as erroneous in its doctrine as well as harmful in its likely effects and roundly declared himself unable to appoint to any parish in Bethnal Green a priest holding such opinions as those expressed therein.

There then ensued between Blomfield and Woodard a protracted and stubborn correspondence, in which the Bishop again and again reiterated his refusal to appoint and license the author of the sermon, while Woodard, with a persistence fully equal to his superior's obstinacy, pleaded his orthodoxy, loyalty to Anglican doctrinal standards, legitimate expectation of preferment and precarious financial position. After a good deal more correspondence, in the course of which Woodard unavailingly summoned the formidable shades of 'the judicious Hooker' and other eminent seventeenth century divines, and even St Chrysostom to testify in his favour, Blomfield equally unavailingly desired that the correspondence might cease. Not so easily, however, are the Woodards of this world deflected from their flint-like courses and the letters continued to fluctuate between Fulham and Bethnal Green.

At length episcopal patience reached the limit of its endurance. Woodard was invited to tender his resignation and to seek a curacy where he might consider himself on probation, what time he purged his doctrine of unacceptable deviations. Such a prospect failing to appeal, Woodard continued respectfully but firmly to importune his diocesan, obtained a personal interview which led nowhere and settled nothing, and wrote yet another lengthy, impassioned appeal the sole result of which was a final curt refusal from Blomfield to appoint him to Bethnal Green. In spite of legal advice that he ought not to resign, Woodard at last found his position no longer tenable, especially as the Bishop had already offered the living of St Bartholomew's to another priest. By way of easing his departure from Bethnal Green Blomfield offered to license him to a curacy at St James's, Clapton, in the near by parish of Hackney, but although the necessities of his economic situation forced Woodard to accept this offer he was far from contented and determined to remove himself from the diocese of London at the first favourable opportunity.

During his period in London Woodard became acquainted with some of the influential men of affairs who were afterwards to be numbered among his most generous and enthusiastic supporters. These included A. J. Beresford-Hope M.P., Henry Tritton the banker, Baron Alderson of the Court of Exchequer, Judge Patteson of the Queen's Bench, and William Cotton, a director and later Governor of the Bank of England. These 'rich men furnished with ability' began by forming an interest in Woodard's religious and philanthropic work amongst the East End poor, became attracted to his personality, and ended as life-long admirers and benefactors of his great educational undertakings. Woodard himself, for all his single-minded intensity of purpose, was far indeed from being a humourless fanatic and appears to have won support for his causes as much by his personal magnetism as by his largeness of outlook and tenacity of aim. He was ever a welcome guest in the houses of the eminent men who backed him and could make himself agreeable in any sort of company by his ease of bearing, unfailing store of anecdotes and friendly, inoffensive badinage.

In London, too, he got to know a young architect of promise, one Richard Carpenter, who, in spite of an untimely death, was later to translate into durable terms of bricks and mortar, stone and flint, many of Woodard's prolific inspirations.

*   *   *

Meanwhile the diocese of London itself seemed a good one to depart from as soon as might be and in 1846, after less than three years at St James's, Clapton, Woodard was offered and accepted an assistant curacy in charge of New Shoreham in Sussex. Shoreham at that time still retained shades of the importance which it had enjoyed as a shipbuilding centre in the sixteenth and seventeenth centuries. Its ancient Norman church, the seafaring atmosphere and the adjacent beauty of the chalk downs acted as tremendous stimulants to Woodard's energy and imagination and he immediately threw himself into his new work with remarkable vigour and enthusiasm.

In Bethnal Green the lack of educational facilities had led him to found a parochial school to help remedy the defect, thus early exhibiting that passion for making Christian learning available to all who desired it and found it hard to come by. The immediate needs of Shoreham in the matter of schools were different from those of Bethnal Green, or at least presented themselves differently to Woodard. Those who here seemed most in want of help were the children of Shoreham's seagoing shipmasters and mates, many of whom sailed in vessels engaged in the coasting trade. For the offspring of these men there were no adequate educational facilities, and Woodard characteristically set to work to supply the want. He appears to have been driven to do so as much by the illiteracy and low moral standard of the Shoreham sea-faring community generally as by their children's intellectual necessities. Before he had been in his new post a year he had begun operations—presumably with the approval of his vicar, William Wheeler, who must have enjoyed progressively less and less parochial assistance from his new lieutenant. Woodard's plan was to provide and establish a grammar school where boys might be taught French, be grounded in the rudiments of navigation, and be instructed in the principles of the Christian Faith.

The first 'Woodard School' was a day school and it was housed in the curate's own dining-room. The master was Charles Christie, a graduate of Queen's College, Oxford, while Woodard supervised the religious instruction and generally acted as chaplain. The fees were £5 a year, and in less than a year after Woodard's arrival in Shoreham the school was in being and filled to its limited capacity. Subscriptions from sympathizers were at once forthcoming to help nourish the growth of this grain of mustard seed from which so noble a tree was to issue, and as the project prospered the scope of Woodard's aims expanded.

The year 1848 was one of unrest and revolution in many countries of Europe. Woodard's heart never failed him but he feared the age of scepticism and contempt for spiritual values which he clearly foresaw was coming upon the earth. One power alone, as he saw it, could stem the march of materialism and that was the power of Christian truth. At the same time only a nation whose leaders, intellectuals, men of affairs and solid middle-class core had received an education securely based upon spiritual principles could hope to possess and wield that power and so save the world and itself from ultimate destruction.

To Woodard the call was rapidly clarifying itself; his life work was taking tangible shape. Shoreham's needs were the needs of the nation. From the window of his parsonage dining-room, where a dozen boys daily bent their heads over French irregular verbs, the theorems of Euclid, the Acts of the Apostles or the Prayer Book Catechism, he looked out and saw in imagination thousands of such boys—parsons' sons, sons of farmers, country doctors, small town attorneys, small tradesmen, military and naval officers—for whom no such Christian education was available at fees their parents could afford. The great public schools had long since ceased to fulfil the purpose for which they had been founded, and had become the exclusive academies of the rich, where only too often religion was nothing more than a matter of conventional observance, accorded without enthusiasm or conviction to the chilly canons of respectability.

So far as the poorer classes were concerned, while the era of State-provided schools was still twenty years in the future, the National Society was doing admirable work in providing elementary education based upon Christian principles. For the lower middle-classes alone there was no provision and to their needs and cause Woodard was to consecrate his outstanding qualities.

*　　*　　*

In 1847 Marx and Engels had issued their famous *Communist Manifesto*, and in the following year Woodard issued his. It bore the curiously modern-sounding title of *A Plea For The Middle Classes* and was altogether a more modest affair than the turgid effusion of the two Germans, but in its own humbler way it dealt with matters of comparable and by no means unconnected import. Marx set out to destroy the middle classes; Woodard, in England at least, to save them. Marx aimed at establishing the dictatorship of the proletariat; Woodard at the recovery of a Christian order of Society— without being much concerned over the purely political or economic issues involved. The conflict between these two incompatible objects has today assumed the proportions of a world struggle.

Woodard's pamphlet outlines his practical purpose as the provision of 'a good and complete education for the middle classes at such a charge as will make it available for most of them.' He stresses the difficulties experienced by the class of people he has in view in educating their sons in a suitable manner and links their problem with their virtual lack of contact with organized religion, referring particularly to the smaller tradesmen and shopkeepers who, he says, were almost entirely neglected by the clergy of the established Church especially in the greater centres of population. A further point which he strongly emphasized was the necessity and urgency of rightly educating those who were to be in turn the teachers of others, especially those who would teach in the elementary parochial schools.

Woodard deals also with the employer class who in mid-Victorian England wielded over their workers an influence which has now largely devolved upon the leaders and officials of the trades unions. He castigates the Church of England of his day for its neglect of those she has received in baptism, and finds the cause of this neglect, not in any want of zeal on the part of the parochial clergy (it was, after all, the great day of the parochial system at its most successful) but in the lack of adequate educational facilities for those potential leaders of men whose circumstances are reduced and financial resources small. It was not enough to educate the masses if those who were to lead, teach or employ them were left in religious ignorance.

'While we spend all our strength upon educating the poor, our forefathers spent theirs on those of the middle ranks,' founding schools which aimed at training them

> in the faith and fear of God, and in such sound principles of knowledge as might fit them to serve their Country in their several stations with the greatest advantage. The two extremes— the rich and the poor—will both find means in abundance for obtaining the education best suited to each. But the middle classes are above charity on the one hand, and on the other as a body cannot give sufficient remuneration to secure competent teachers when the Church withdraws her help.[1]

Woodard then proceeds to expound his plan.

The Church should be in a position to offer a boarding school education at a lower charge than other schools of a similar type which were more concerned with material manifestations of prosperity than with the spiritual well-being of

[1]Otter—pp. 43–44.

their pupils. To ensure that the spiritual aims of the schools should not be lost sight of, masters in responsible positions were to be in Holy Orders. Fellows of Oxford and Cambridge Colleges with adequate incomes and nominal duties were to be invited to offer their assistance for the good of the cause—an astute move which met with some success.

At first, two types of school were envisaged, but later a third type was included in the general scheme. The costs of maintenance were minutely gone into, and Woodard maintained that it would be possible to provide board, lodging and education in the cheaper type of school for as little as £14 a year, though the fees in the better sort of school, from which it was hoped to recruit a good part of the teaching staff for the second group of schools, would naturally be somewhat higher. Those were the days when 'private means' were not yet taxed out of existence and Woodard expected that many would be found able and willing to give their teaching services without remuneration other than board and lodging.

The *Plea for the Middle Classes*, poorly printed and unattractive in appearance though we are told it was, proved to be the Charter of Christian Middle Class Education and a tract for the times as powerful in its effects as those which had in the preceding decade flowed from the pens of the Oxford Fathers. Privately circulated among a wide and influential range of men in public life—political, commercial, ecclesiastical and academic—it met at once with a gratifying response. W. E. Gladstone —then a rising young Tory statesman—J. B. Mozley, Charles Marriott, Archdeacon Manning, and Edward Bouverie Pusey were among those who expressed approval of the plan, as did the Dean and Archdeacons of Woodard's own diocese of Chichester. Magdalen College, patron of the livings of Old and New Shoreham, as well as of others in the neighbourhood, took an interest in the scheme and came forward with the offer of a substantial grant.

★   ★   ★

Woodard wasted no time before he went into action. Houses in Shoreham were leased as temporary quarters for the first boarding school, called to begin with 'Shoreham Grammar

School' and afterwards rechristened 'St Nicolas College'. The maximum fee was to be £40 a year and the minimum £30.

The fame of Woodard's new venture rapidly circulated and requests began to reach him to open similar schools in various parts of the country. Nothing would have gratified him more than to be in a position to do so, but at the moment he had more than enough to occupy his mind. His immediate objective was to found three schools in Sussex and to this end he launched the 'Society of St Nicolas' for 'the education of the sons of the middle classes at such terms as will make education available for most of them'. Reluctant though he was at first to do so, he finally yielded to pressure and assumed control of the young society and its work under the title of Provost.

It was a further part of his plan that some at least of the masters in the schools should be produced by the society itself and to this end he proposed a system of Fellowships to be held for eight years, of which the first four would be probationary. During the second four-year period those who survived would be required to hold themselves in readiness to teach in any school of the society to which they might be sent. Thus, he felt a true team spirit would be engendered to the inestimable advantage both of teachers and taught.

St Nicolas' Grammar School was opened on 1 August 1848, in the presence of a considerable number of friends and supporters. The first headmaster was the Reverend Henry Jacobs, Michel Fellow of Queen's College, Oxford. He, however, only stayed for one term, failing to see eye to eye with Woodard on certain points which the latter insisted upon as fundamental, notably the independent position of the chaplain as guardian of the faith and morals of the boys.

He was succeeded by C. E. Moberly of Balliol, whose teaching gifts proved greater than his attachment to the ideals of the Society for in 1851 he resigned, after having been involved in negotiations for the headmastership of another school. This, to Woodard, savoured of duplicity, if not treason, and he felt let down and disappointed at what he considered Moberly's want of a sense of corporate loyalty. His successor was John Braithwaite, another Fellow of Queen's College, Oxford.

The second stage of Woodard's plan was put into operation in 1859 when a second-grade school was opened in hired houses in Shoreham, under the headmastership of the Reverend Edward Lowe, until then curate of Ottery St Mary. Lowe was a man of considerable ability, and was to prove himself thoroughly in harmony with the Founder's aims and methods. As a master he knew his job, but because of his autocratic bearing and occasional outbursts of violent anger he was probably respected rather than loved by his pupils. He became the Founder's right-hand man and devoted admirer, and the rest of his life was spent in the service of the Society. In 1872 he was appointed the first Provost of Denstone, and after Woodard's death he was elected Provost of Lancing.

*   *   *

Woodard's earlier differences with Bishop Blomfield of London resulted in no personal ill-will between the two men and in February 1850 the bishop invited his former subordinate to extend his activities by the foundation of schools in the diocese of London. To this end he offered to place at Woodard's disposal the organization and funds of his existing Diocesan Association for Education and also to contribute further sums from his own pocket. Woodard at first seems to have received the proposal with some degree of enthusiasm and gratification, and to have envisaged forthwith a network of schools for the middle classes of the metropolis complementary to those provided by the National Society for the Education of the Poor. Nothing, however, came of the project, though why this should have been so is not now easy to determine. What probably diverted Woodard's mind at the time was his complete pre-occupation with the work already in hand, and ultimately the deciding factor may have been his growing conviction that his schools could best flourish in comparatively remote places, removed from the distractions and competing claims of busy urban surroundings. But at least the episode is a clear indication that Blomfield's former distrust of Woodard's teaching and churchmanship was by this time largely dissipated.

The Provost's next experiment was a military and engineer-

· ing school, established about this time at Leyton for candidates for commissions in the Army. One of the Hurstpierpoint masters, F. M. Arnold, was appointed as Head of this new venture which was primarily, though not exclusively, intended to provide a semi-professional preparatory training for boys who had passed through the school at Shoreham. The fees were £60 a year and visiting lecturers from London and elsewhere were engaged. This school functioned successfully for seven years before finally closing for want of sufficient entrants.

The rapid growth and expanding possibilities of his educational projects had by now made it practically impossible to attend at all satisfactorily to his parochial duties, and in 1850 he resigned from the curacy of New Shoreham. His brief period spent in the service of the parish had left a deep impression, more particularly upon the seafaring section of the community, whose educational needs had first kindled the fire of his creative genius, and his departure occasioned much sincere regret.

Suggestions for the extension of his scheme continued to reach Woodard from many quarters, and with them came fresh recruits to assist him in the promotion of his aims. The work was rapidly developing in scope far beyond the capacities of one man, unaided, to develop and control, and its ultimate success was in no small part due to the quality and loyalty of the men who became his lieutenants. It could have grown more rapidly still had a serious attempt been made by the authorities of the various dioceses to provide schools similar to those at Shoreham and Hurstpierpoint, merely looking to Woodard, perhaps, for general advice and supervision. But no such concerted effort was made; the call to initiate and organize was addressed in each case to him personally, and to respond to so many requests was beyond the powers of any one man however exceptional his gifts and energy. His three schools in Sussex were as much as he was able to cope with at the moment, though he did at this time (1850) offer to buy an Agricultural College at Cirencester and actually entered into negotiations for the founding of schools in at least two other dioceses.

His astonishing *flair* for raising large sums of money induced envy in some and admiration in many, and was firmly based upon his uncompromising appeal to a sense of obligation on the part of churchmen possessed of the means to give generously and without thought of personal profit, reputation or reward. But not to the largest and most faithful of the schools' benefactors did he ever consent to yield any portion of his controlling power.

*   *   *

A great step forward in Woodard's work was taken on 15 June 1851, when the foundation stone of the school at Hurstpierpoint was laid by the Bishop of Chichester, Ashurst Gilbert, in the presence of a large and distinguished gathering.

In the late autumn of that same year Woodard compiled an open letter to the clergy of the diocese of Chichester, to each member of which he sent a copy. In this epistle he summarized the prevailing state of religion (or irreligion), especially drawing attention to its dangers and drawbacks to the work of Christian education. He then proceeded to explain his great project of founding Church boarding schools of three distinct grades, in all of which the Christian Faith would occupy a central and decisive position. The work of their chaplains was to be all-important and pre-eminently spiritual in its scope, for with his customary acumen Woodard saw how easily the desirable pastoral relationship between the boys and those entrusted with the care of their souls could be hampered and even destroyed by treating chaplains merely as ordained masters and requiring them to fill their days with secular instruction and the maintenance of discipline—a false economy of which not even the armed forces of the Crown were guilty.

> Another feature of the plan is that there should be chaplains appointed to these schools; because we think that a greater degree of confidence will be inspired by a clergyman who has nothing to do with teaching and punishing; and because in after life, these children will love us more for having taken care of their souls, than for anything we may have taught them either of technical religion or of science.

In 1852 Woodard followed up his open letter of the previous year with a pamphlet entitled *Public Schools for the Middle Classes* in which he repeated the arguments already advanced

in his *Plea for the Middle Classes* but this time with a more pronounced political twist and with special reference to the
question of parliamentary franchise, at that time a matter of
considerable public controversy. Woodard was deeply concerned to ensure that when universal suffrage came, as he
clearly foresaw it must, it should be bestowed upon an electorate
mentally, morally and spiritually educated and equipped to
make responsible and conscientious use of it. To this desirable
end the schools he was founding would, he felt certain, make
their not-unimportant contribution.

The new school at Hurstpierpoint was opened on 21 June
1853, and the preacher on this occasion was Connop Thirlwall,
Bishop of St David's. The collection taken at the service reached
the handsome total of £600, but as the Provost subsequently
entertained to luncheon between five and six hundred guests,
including many persons of substance and standing, this result
was not perhaps so surprising as it may sound to modern ears
accustomed to less liberal benefactions. Among those present at
the opening ceremony and luncheon were the Bishops of
Chichester and Exeter (Phillpotts), Archdeacon Hare (who
sided with the Privy Council against Phillpotts over the Gorham affair—one wonders if they were neighbours at the
luncheon table!), the Duke of Buccleuch, A. J. Beresford-Hope,
M.P., Lord Downs, W. Sewell (founder of Radley), J. G.
Hubbard, H. P. Liddon of St Paul's, Lord Robert Cecil (later
to become the third Marquess of Salisbury and famous Conservative Foreign Secretary and Prime Minister) and representatives of five Oxford Colleges. Lord Robert was to become
one of Woodard's warmest supporters, a trustee of St Nicolas'
College, and until increasing political activities prevented him
from doing so he took an active and important part in the
promotion of the Provost's schemes.

The school buildings were designed by Richard Carpenter
in the Decorated Gothic style, and were constructed from split
flints and Caen stone. The situation selected was remarkable
both for its seclusion and its beauty and was described by Keble,
perhaps a trifle ambiguously, as 'a place to live and die in'.

* * *

B.B.—H

About this time Woodard received valuable support and encouragement from other prominent men, among them Sidney Herbert, Secretary of State for War, Charles Kingsley, Lord Redesdale and Lord John Manners. As a special compliment to the Provost, Herbert presented his eldest son Mortimer with a commission in the Army without the purchase then customary.

A 'London Committee' had been formed some short time previously, with Lord Robert Cecil as chairman, to extend and make more widely known the work of St Nicolas' College; but this body, consisting as it did of most of Woodard's influential city and political friends, proved too large and cumbersome for real efficiency and on Lord Robert's suggestion a small executive committee was appointed with satisfactory results. Local committees were also formed in Oxford, Cambridge, Brighton, Lewes, Shoreham, Hurstpierpoint, Cuckfield and Bognor; from which it will be seen that, London and the universities apart, a large proportion of Woodard's support was still forthcoming from the county of Sussex and depended mainly upon the magnetic quality and powerful personality of the Founder himself. His gifts of eloquence, persuasion and burning sincerity swayed the minds and touched the hearts of his hearers, kindling their imagination and leading them to give with such astonishing generosity. Other men in the nineteenth century achieved remarkable results in raising funds for causes of a purely charitable nature, but there is probably no parallel for the response which Woodard wooed from the wills and pockets of hard-headed men of commerce and public affairs in the interest of a cause which was almost entirely lacking in popular, sentimental appeal and which called for, on the part of its supporters, religious conviction, clarity of thought and an uncommon length of view. Those are the criteria by which must be assessed the extent of Woodard's achievements and the true measure of his greatness.

On 4 April 1855, Woodard executed a Deed of Trust in respect of the property of his Society and this Deed, the trustees of which were Lord Robert Cecil, Sir John Patteson, Henry Tritton, A. J. Beresford-Hope, and J. G. Hubbard, afterwards the first Lord Addington, was duly enrolled in Chancery. It begins with an invocation of the Holy Trinity and a characteristic preamble compiled by the Provost personally. It may be said to epitomize for posterity his deepest faith, most cherished ideals and life-long endeavour.

It being my earnest wish, and the object and intention of all the benefactors of the Corporation of SS Mary and Nicolas, that for all future time the sons of any of Her Majesty's subjects should be taught, together with sound Grammar learning, the fear and honour of the Almighty God, the Father, the Son, and the Holy Ghost, according to the doctrines of the Catholic Faith as it is now set forth in the Book of the Offices and Administration of the Sacraments of the Church of England.

And I charge every member of the said Corporation to use his utmost influence to defend and protect these our wishes and intentions, for the glory of God, the exaltation of the Faith, and the blessedness of our fellow-subjects, as he or they shall answer the same at the Day of Judgment. And be it further understood, that in laying this obligation, under the most solemn objurgations, upon the members of the Corporation, by virtue of the powers reserved to me in the afore-named Deeds, I do it also in the name and by the wishes of many thousand good and self-denying Catholic Christians, who have united with me in this work out of love for the souls of their fellow-creatures, and from motives of true patriotism towards their Country.

And I implore the Civil Government, of whatever sort it may be, to respect the rights of property and of conscience, and not to set aside these my Statutes, which are given to secure the teaching of the Christian Faith, pure and unadulterated, as we in England now enjoy it.

The Statutes upon which the constitution of 'The Society of SS Mary and Nicolas, Lancing' rests were not finally promulgated until 1880, after many tentative drafts had been made. The Founder had at one time thought of applying for incorporation under Royal Charter and at another under Act of Parliament, but his dislike of State influence and interference to even a moderate degree finally decided him against adopting either course and his foundation was to remain independent and unfettered. Later, other divisional societies were formed under their own Provosts and Fellows and brought into federal union under the comprehensive title of 'The Corporation of SS Mary and Nicolas'.

★   ★   ★

The first stone of Lancing College had been laid privately on St Benedict's Day, 21 March 1854; the public ceremony being postponed until 4 July in the following year when the foundation stone was laid by Sir John Patteson, the senior trustee. The sermon on this occasion was preached by Arthur Stanley, later Dean of Westminster. In purchasing nearly one hundred and fifty acres of land on the south-eastern slopes of the Downs above Shoreham the Provost had planned the building, not only of the Lancing College that was to be, but also of a permanent home and headquarters for the Society, a conception as splendid as the Sussex scenery amidst which it was to be realized. Hurstpierpoint, still uncompleted and without a chapel or headmaster's house, had already cost £40,000, but with faith undaunted and unbelievable courage he nevertheless launched out without delay upon his immeasurably vaster and more costly enterprise. His faith was justified, his courage rewarded. The money came in—large sums from such generous and loyal supporters as Henry Tritton, J. G. Hubbard and the Bishop of Chichester; smaller but no less welcome amounts from a multitude of folk of more moderate means who had likewise caught something of the Founder's vision and burning zeal.

It should be borne in mind that all this generous giving was for capital expenditure only. Woodard was not founding charitable institutions to be dependent on public subscription. He asked only for sufficient money to start his schools; it was his intention from the first that once on their feet they should be self-supporting in their service of Christian education, and this the Woodard schools have ever successfully been in spite of the fact that fees have always been kept as low as is consistent with solvency. At Ardingly, when it was opened in 1870, the fees for full board and tuition were only fifteen guineas a year, a figure made possible to no small extent by the fact that many of the teaching staff, graduates of Oxford and Cambridge and men of private means, responded nobly to the Provost's appeal and gave their services for many years for a bare pittance. Such was the devotion and sacrifice which Woodard inspired among many of the best of contemporary Christian educationalists. His was a gift which, had his lines been differently cast, might well have made him the successful leader of apparently forlorn hopes and reputedly lost causes. Woodard's sober priestly garb and Garibaldi's revolutionary red shirt were worn by men of not dissimilar mould. It was this rare quality to which Mr Gladstone referred in a letter to the Provost, enclosing a donation and dated 3 July 1856, in which the future Prime Minister professes himself to be 'under the resistless influence and admiration which zeal, energy and sagacity like yours, and so directed, cannot fail to excite'.

Unfortunately, zeal, energy and even sagacity have a way of exciting as much hostility from opponents as admiration from friends, and Woodard came in for a plentiful spate of criticism and opposition from those whose prejudices were offended by his convinced and uncompromising Church principles. On 2 December 1856, a meeting was arranged to take place in the Brighton Town Hall, in support of St Nicholas' College, with Lord Robert Cecil in the chair. It was made the occasion of a violent 'anti-Puseyite' demonstration, ably organized by a certain Protestant agitator of the name of Foskett who packed the hall with his supporters long before the meeting was due to begin, thus effectively excluding the bulk of Woodard's backers and well-wishers. The proceedings were conducted against a background of hostile comment, constant interruption, groans, hisses and vulgar insults. More than one speaker, including the Bishop of the diocese, was shouted down, and the meeting ended in disorder and uproar with the angry mob storming the platform and Foskett shouting hysterically, 'Thanks be to God, Who giveth us the victory'. But Foskett's victory began and ended on the platform of Brighton Town Hall. Decent people viewed such antics with disgust and Woodard won many new adherents in consequence.

Such irritations, however, were merely incidental to the main business of establishing the schools and in this same year of 1857 the move was made from New Shoreham Vicarage which was now required by a new incumbent, the Upper School moving first, the Lower School in the following year. Only the north and south sides of the first quadrangle, the lower hall and the walls of the upper hall had been completed when the transfer was made in July, and much additional expenditure, originally budgeted for the following year, was necessary to enable the school to function in its new and permanent surroundings by the beginning of the autumn term. As Lancing was to provide the headquarters of the Corporation as well as housing St Nicolas' College, the buildings were planned on a generous scale. It was intended that members of other schools should meet at Lancing once or twice a year, and the hall was designed to hold some fifteen hundred boys.

A third-grade school, under the title of St Saviour's College, was founded in the buildings vacated at Shoreham. One of the assistant masters at Lancing, Frederic Mertens of Queen's College, Oxford, was the first headmaster, and the fees were fixed at thirteen guineas a year, inclusive of tuition, board and lodging. In July 1870 St Saviour's College was transferred to Ardingly, and the fees were increased to fifteen guineas per annum.

*   *   *

Further projects and propositions soon presented themselves for Woodard's active consideration, either unsought from without or as the consequence of his own fertile cogitations.

In 1858 a school at Bloxham, near Banbury, which had been begun by a Mr Hewett, was offered to Woodard for £5,000. The Provost regarded this apparently reasonable price as excessive and declined the offer. Two or three years later it changed hands for the incredibly low figure of £1,500 and the purchaser, Philip Egerton, Fellow of New College, Oxford, proposed that it should be taken over as part of the Corporation of St Nicolas. The terms, however, under which the transfer was to be made did not commend themselves to Woodard and it was not until 1896, after many unavailing attempts on the part of Egerton to induce the Provost to accept responsibility, that the school was finally and unconditionally transferred to the Corporation. By this time more than £30,000 had been spent on the buildings, originally designed by the prominent architect George Edmund Street. From 1865 to 1878 the chaplain and second master was the Reverend A. D. Crake, in his day a well-known writer of juvenile historical fiction.

A project of Woodard's own conceiving was the foundation of a college for missionaries of every kind and calling—priests, teachers, scholars, architects, engineers, craftsmen—to be attached to St Saviour's College at Ardingly. This ambitious plan aimed at providing trained recruits of every description to meet the needs of the Church overseas, and was to be complementary to the department for training schoolmasters planned as part of the establishment at Hurstpierpoint. It was soon seen, however, that to try to combine a school for boys with a training college for young men was not practicable and the idea was not persisted in.

It was now apparent that the accommodation at Shoreham was quite inadequate to meet the requirements of the rapidly-growing 'lower-middle' or third-grade school, and Woodard began to seek a suitable site on which to build. In 1861 he was able to buy 200 acres of land in the parish of Ardingly, and to raise the funds to make the purchase he planned two great public meetings, one in London and the other at Oxford. His existing resources were strained to the utmost by the work already in hand at Lancing and at Hurstpierpoint, and the need for new subscribers had become imperative. Woodard had strict views with regard to money matters. He had had it laid down in the trust deeds that the Society's property should at no time be mortgaged, nor would he ever consent to the incurring of debts which he saw no immediate prospect of discharging. On the strength of promises from persons of integrity and good standing, however, he would arrange for large overdrafts from the banking concern of which his loyal friend and generous supporter, Henry Tritton, was an active partner.

The London meeting, held in St James's Hall on 8 June 1861, was filled to capacity and proved a tremendous success. The aged statesman, Lord Brougham, presided and the very distinguished 'platform' included Archbishop Longley of York (later of Canterbury), Lord John Manners, the Bishop of

Chichester, George Augustus Sala, John Walter of *The Times*, Lord Redesdale, Sir W. Page Wood (afterwards Lord Chancellor) and Lord Lyttelton. Bishop Wilberforce of Oxford, who was unable to be present, wrote: 'If you have the opportunity pray express the strength of my conviction that upon this question of middle-class education does at this moment absolutely hang the future destinies of our land, and that I believe you have done more than any man living to give the question its true solution.' The meeting was fully reported in the national press, and *The Times* and the *Standard* both devoted leading articles to extolling the aims and importance of the movement.

Although he had been oddly reluctant to do so, Woodard himself laid the foundation stone of the chapel at Hurstpierpoint on the 17 September 1861. The Provost seems to have attached an almost disproportionate significance to these stone-laying ceremonies, and it is indicative of the man's innate modesty that he should consider himself unworthy to perform one of them and that it should have required the combined pressure of his friends and the insistence of his diocesan to persuade him to do so on this occasion. So averse was he to even a suggestion of self-glorification or publicity that he rigidly refused to speak either at the great summer meeting at St James's Hall or at the subsequent one in the Oxford Sheldonian—to the intense disappointment of the audience at both gatherings. Bishop Wilberforce was able to be present at the Hurstpierpoint stone-laying and preached a sermon which was listened to with enthralled attention, even by the boys.

For the meeting at Oxford in the Sheldonian theatre Woodard, with his usual skill in enlisting the active support of the prominent and influential, not only persuaded the Vice-Chancellor (Jeune, Master of Pembroke) to preside but secured as his principal speakers the two greatest oratorical 'draws' of their day, Bishop Samuel Wilberforce and Mr W. E. Gladstone. The nearest equivalent in more recent years would have been Sir Winston Churchill and Archbishop Temple speaking from the same platform and it is almost impossible to doubt that Woodard, had he been their contemporary, would have been successful in securing their joint appearance! Gladstone at that time was Member of Parliament for Oxford University and Chancellor of the Exchequer, and Lord Robert Cecil, who asked to be excused from making a speech on this occasion, expressed in a letter to Woodard his astonished admiration at the Provost's pertinacity and skill in persuading such eminent personalities to speak in support of his projects.

The meeting was attended by nearly all the Heads of Houses, numerous dons and undergraduates, the Mayor of Oxford and representatives of the City Corporation, and the Sheldonian Theatre was packed. There was one notable absentee—Dr Pusey, who had ceased to attend public meetings.

There was an attempt on the part of the egregious Mr Golightly[1] of Oriel and his followers to discredit Woodard and his work before the meeting began. People arriving at the theatre were handed leaflets purporting to reveal the 'Romanizing' tendencies of St Nicolas' College. The Vice-Chancellor, after scornful reference to the misrepresentations contained in these prejudiced pamphlets, spoke of Woodard as an extraordinary man who had risen among them, gifted with the power of governing others and with the talent for inspiring them with his own generous ideals.

Mr Gladstone, in a long and heavily eloquent speech, moved 'That considering the growth of intelligence among the lower classes and owing to the impulse given of late years to education, the establishment of public boarding-schools for the education of the lower middle-class which may be cheap and self-supporting is of great national importance'. The famous Chancellor and future Prime Minister appears to have been at his most Gladstonian, and doubtless Queen Victoria—had her Majesty unaccountably been present—would not have been even mildly amused. She would probably have enjoyed more the Bishop of Oxford's witty and felicitous speech which was received with delighted acclamation by his enthusiastic audience.

The meeting was altogether a huge success, and Woodard was deeply gratified to feel that the foremost centre of English

[1]Pleasingly known in Oxford as 'Agag', he who 'went delicately'. But Golightly, it would appear, was a man of girth.

learning should thus have bestowed its blessing upon his aims and labours.

★   ★   ★

The laying of the Ardingly foundation stone took place on 12 July 1864—yet another of those impressive functions, rounded off by a sumptuous luncheon, in which the Provost delighted and which in the piping days of Victorian plenty were so prominent a feature of Woodard social life and hospitality. 'Nice luncheons' (to use Lord Robert Cecil's phrase) were, in fact, one of the Provost's favourite propagandist and money-raising devices, a circumstance to which ill-wishers (and the uninvited) were occasionally wont to make soured and disparaging reference. Nevertheless, no great occasion—such as a stone-laying or opening ceremony—was considered complete unless concluded by one of these banquets, and if hundreds at a time enjoyed Woodard's hospitality the cost was insignificant compared with the extra money they invariably brought in by way of donations and subscriptions. The Provost, perhaps a shade cynically but with some psychological insight, believed that a rich man's palate was one way to his purse.

Ardingly stands amidst what is considered by some the loveliest scenery surrounding any of the Woodard schools. It occupies one of the southern slopes of the forest ridges, flanked by bosky woodlands and with one of two small but delightful lakes adorning the rich pasturelands between the school and the valley of the Sussex Ouse half a mile or so distant. The other lake lies a little to the north, hidden in a fold of the hills, at the foot of the forest ridge. The Founder bought and chose well in purchasing the Ardingly estate and in his selection of position for the buildings of the school.

The stone was laid by Earl Granville, Lord President of the Council, who at that time exercised the functions, such as they were, of Minister of Education. It was on account of this latter aspect of his office that he had been invited to perform the ceremony, and as he had previously shown little or no interest in Woodard's projects a certain amount of judicious 'priming' on the part of Lord Lyttelton and others had been necessary to make him *au fait* with what was being aimed at and with what had already been accomplished. Granville, good easy man but shrewd and diplomatic, appears to have mastered his briefing and to have been duly appreciative of what he had read, heard and seen. At the luncheon he amiably twitted the Provost upon his disparagement of his own achievements, and expressed the curious opinion that the universities should carry on the work which Woodard had begun. History fails to record Woodard's reaction to that remarkable suggestion.

Old Lord Brougham, then 86 years of age, and the Bishop of Oxford also spoke; as did Lord Robert Cecil, who described himself as having been an intruder and charity boy at school and university, for both the places of learning he had attended were originally intended for that very class which the Woodard Foundations were seeking to benefit. That class had long since been pushed out by the powerful and wealthy, and restitution was overdue—a striking statement which must have occasioned considerably more serious thought and searchings of heart than the Lord President's well-meant but misty meanderings. As for the Provost, he appears to have enjoyed himself hugely; and as he surveyed the assembled company he is said to have observed astringently, 'This is like Heaven. Many whom I confidently expect to meet are absent, and many more surprise me by their presence'.

By this time he was able to command considerable support in high places. Archbishop Longley, Archbishop Trench of Dublin, the future Archbishop Frederick Temple (then Head-master of Rugby) and most of the English bishops approved of his aims; while an old friend, Professor Montague Burrows, wrote: 'It is the obvious work of the day, and it is only wonderful that it has not been taken in hand before. Your success will soon be followed up by others, and the middle classes will once more become the strength of the Church'. To whatever extent this enthusiastic prophecy may be thought to have been fulfilled, Woodard must undoubtedly receive no insignificant portion of the credit due.

Following the Ardingly foundation stone-laying, the next great function was the opening of the chapel at Hurstpierpoint on the 17 October 1865. The chapel, built in the 'geometrical

Gothic style of split flints and Caen stone, was designed by Richard Cromwell Carpenter and after his death the work was carried out by his son, Richard Herbert, who had succeeded him, in partnership with William Slater, as architect to the Society. *The Guardian* newspaper described the chapel as 'one of the noblest efforts of ecclesiastical art that have yet been set on foot, even in these days of church-building and restoration'. The sermon, preached by the spell-binding H. P. Liddon, lasted over an hour, but Victorian church-goers were cast in a more heroic mould than their modern counterparts as far as preachings were concerned, and possibly the only discontent at the length of Liddon's discourse was experienced by the boys. The invited guests, at least, were able to refresh their flagging spirits at the inevitable luncheon which followed, when the Provost made a passionate appeal for yet more financial and practical help. He was ably seconded by the ever-faithful Lord Robert (Cecil) and Beresford-Hope, who said that the occasion marked the consummation of one of the most courageous movements of the day—the first great proclamation to England that her middle classes did still belong to the English Church; that the Church of England had not yet become a select club for the upper classes, or a blanket dispensary and soup-kitchen for the poor—but that the English Church represented the Catholic Faith in this land, and that the English Church was, ought to be, and should be the Church of the great middle classes of the English people.

★   ★   ★

Work was now in full swing at Ardingly. More new buildings were needed at Lancing; and at Hurstpierpoint, the chapel having been completed, it was immediately necessary to provide a house for the headmaster. But in spite of these very considerable commitments Woodard's aims continued to embrace ever-widening horizons, and from Sussex he turned his attention to the Midlands. The financial resources of the Society were already extended to the limits of safety, his health was impaired by the magnitude of the existing projects for whose direction and completion he held himself personally responsible. It

accordingly seemed to this remarkable man an opportune
moment to launch out upon a fresh and formidable undertaking.

He had already attracted the attention and support of a
number of influential people in the Midlands, amongst them the
Earl of Shrewsbury, Sir Percival Heywood, Henry Meynell,
Vicar of Denstone (Staffordshire); O. E. Coope, head of a well-
known Burton brewing concern; George Mackarness, Vicar of
Ilam and afterwards Bishop of Argyll and the Isles; and John
Lonsdale, Bishop of Lichfield, who warmly welcomed Woodard
and his Society within his diocese. A site for a school was offered
by Sir Percival Heywood in the parish of Denstone (some four
miles from the little market town of Uttoxeter), together with
an extremely generous donation, in memory of a son who had
recently died. Woodard gratefully accepted this offer and at
once sought and obtained the permission of the Bishop to open
a school in the diocese of Lichfield. This school was also to be
the administrative headquarters of the Midland division
(dedicated to St Mary and St John of Lichfield) of the Corporation, the first step in the Provost's cherished plan of regional
divisions; each under its own Provost and enjoying full autonomy, but working alongside the parent Society in the unity of
the entire Corporation. The school itself was to be placed under
the patronage of the first and greatest of all the bishops of
Lichfield—the holy St Chad. The site possessed most if not
all of the Provost's well-known requirements; remoteness,
spaciousness and natural beauty were amongst its undoubted
characteristics, though in its wild, wind-swept situation the
semi-cultivated charm of the softer, sheltered Sussex landscape
was noticeably lacking.

There was a certain amount of Protestant opposition, the
flames of which were fanned by some of the local newspapers,
but it was of small consequence and in no way hindered the
progress of the new school. The foundation stone was laid on
22 October 1868, by Canon Lonsdale (son of the late Bishop of
Lichfield), deputizing for Lord Salisbury who had promised to
perform the ceremony but had been taken suddenly ill. The
Earl of Shrewsbury, who four years later presented the school

with its hall, provided hospitality at Ingestre and Alton Towers
for those invited to the ceremony. At the subsequent luncheon
J. G. Hubbard said, amidst great applause:

> Mr Woodard has taught me to look upon education as the
> training of the whole child till he become the man, fitted at once
> for his secular and social duties, and for that higher sphere of
> existence to which he is destined as an immortal being. . . .
>
> Religious education to be effective must be education con-
> ducted by sincere and earnest men. And who can be a sincere and
> earnest man unless he has a strong and definite faith, which he
> feels it is his duty to impart to those under his care?[1]

St Chad's College, Denstone, was opened in 1873, the fore-
runner of that important group of schools forming the Midland
Division of the Woodard Corporation which now contains a
greater number of schools than any of the other three groups—
the Southern, Western and Northern Divisions. The chapel was
dedicated in 1887, when Archbishop Benson of Canterbury was
the preacher, and the collection amounted to £1,500. The
dining-hall was not completed until the year of the Founder's
death (1891), by which time close on £100,000 had been spent
on the buildings. Since then there must have been considerable
important additions—gymnasium, sanatorium, laboratories,
drill hall, music school, new classrooms, etc.—and, for all its
'Victorian Gothic' appearance and the fact that it remains
tiresomely difficult of access even in this over-mechanized age,
Denstone embodies in its sturdy framework a fitting memorial
in the Midlands to the man whose mind conceived it, and in the
nearly eighty years of its history has come to occupy a place of
importance and esteem, not only within the fellowship of the
Woodard Foundations, but amongst the leading and recognized public schools of the land.

*   *   *

Plans were now forming in the Provost's mind for more new
schools in association with Denstone, although he was suffering
seriously from overwork, largely on account of the urgent necessity of frequent visits to the Midlands. Building at Ardingly

[1]Otter—p. 221.

was going rapidly ahead and during 1868 Woodard intended to begin the new chapel at Lancing. The immediate difficulty was lack of funds for only enough money was as yet available for the actual foundations. This, however, never seems to have deterred the Provost and arrangements were soon on foot for the laying of the foundation stone.

The plans of the chapel came in for a good deal of criticism on utilitarian grounds, the critics considering that the whole scheme was too grandiose and that a smaller erection would have served the school's needs adequately. Woodard, however, was adamant; he was set upon a chapel which should not only be capable of accommodating vast congregations drawn, on special occasions, from all the schools and their supporters—a kind of Corporation Cathedral, as it were—but should also stand as an impressive symbol of the spiritual purpose under-lying the Founder's educational ventures. The intention was entirely admirable, and if one can with difficulty avoid the feeling that in their pious enthusiasm the Victorian church-builders sometimes forgot the burden of upkeep which would fall upon those who came after, one ought not, perhaps, to blame them too much for failing to see an era when even the erection of scaffolding for the replacing of a few tiles or slates from a church roof may involve those responsible in an expendi-ture of several hundred pounds.

Woodard, of course, never saw Lancing Chapel completed, nor can he have expected to do so. Indeed, it remains un-completed still. The foundation stone was laid on 18 July 1868, by Bishop Gilbert of Chichester. The crypt was opened as a temporary chapel in 1875, while the main body of the building —choir and side isles—was opened for services in 1911. This is not the place to give a detailed description of this magnificent edifice; suffice it to say that it has been described as 'the most perfect example of English church architecture since the Re-formation'—extravagant praise, perhaps, when one recollects the name of Wren, but the relative merits of the Gothic and the Classical styles must ever be a matter for the experts to debate and for the rest of us to get heated about. Woodard had had no architectural training and possessed no technical knowledge or skill. But his was the eye of the natural artist and Richard Carpenter, the designer of the chapel, fully shared his ideals, Lancing Chapel represents the vision of the one wedded to the skill of the other.

In March 1870, the Prime Minister, Mr Gladstone, wrote to Woodard offering him a Canonry at Manchester, and Woodard accepted the offer, feeling that the proffered post would provide him with the valuable opportunities for extending his educational aims in the North and Midlands without encroaching unduly upon the time he needed to pursue them. Another honour which came to the Provost in that year, and one which greatly gratified him, was the conferring upon him by the University of Oxford of the Honorary Degree of D.C.L. The distinction was received at the hands of the Chancellor of the University at the Encaenia in June, when others similarly honoured included H. P. Liddon, Matthew Arnold and Lord Lyttelton. This double dignity in one and the same year was a matter of deep satisfaction to Woodard, who saw reason to regard it as recognition in the highest quarters of the value and importance of the work of his schools.

No sooner was he installed in Manchester than he began to advocate in that city the claims of his cause. He accepted invitations to many dinners and other social engagements which he felt might lead to useful connexions and future support, earning thereby the commiseration of Lord Salisbury who described death by slow indigestion as an exquisite form of martyrdom unknown to the ancient persecutors of the Church. Woodard planned a great meeting to be held in the Free Trade Hall, but he quickly discovered that in Manchester there were fresh forms of opposition to be encountered and overcome. The Church Association, a particularly prejudiced Low Church organization, proceeded to stimulate party antagonism by publishing and widely distributing a pamphlet bitterly hostile to the Woodard schools. The new Bishop, James Fraser, also proved to be obstructive, criticizing the Provost's scheme as 'monarchical and sacerdotal' and advising that the projected meeting be postponed. He was clearly apprehensive lest there should be an outbreak of party strife in a city and diocese and county where feelings on such matters have always tended to be easily aroused and to run high. To be the cause of such strife was utterly repugnant to the Provost and in deference to his superior's wishes he postponed the meeting.

The following year he launched a formal appeal for support in founding a 'Midland Counties and Manchester Public School for the Sons of Persons of small means', which was to accommodate 1,000 boys and the fees of which would not be above fifteen guineas a year. His idea was to form a committee of prominent persons in the city and diocese and he wrote to the Bishop inviting him to serve upon it. Perhaps not unnaturally, his lordship, while expressing his admiration for the Provost's zeal and enthusiasm, declared himself unwilling to act with a committee over whose proceedings one man, and that man one of his own subordinates, claimed a right of veto. Nor did he feel that his views and Woodard's on points of Churchmanship would be likely to coincide. The scheme accordingly had to go forward without the backing of the diocesan bishop, but although there was so marked a divergence between Woodard and his superior, their mutual respect and friendship were in no way impaired.

In his search for a suitable situation for the school which was to benefit the Manchester folk whom he had already persuaded to support it so extensively, Woodard considered sites at Crewe, Knutsford, Shavington and Hawarden, but the site eventually settled upon was at Ellesmere in Shropshire, upon sixty acres of land sold at a low price by Lord Brownlow who also contributed £1,000 towards the building fund. The position is a good one in the midst of pleasant pastoral country, with an admirable view of the distant Llangollen hills. The foundation stone was laid by Lord and Lady Brownlow on St Oswald's Day, 5 August 1879, in honour of that Saxon king and martyr who is said to have been slain in battle against the Mercian hordes of heathen Penda at the Battle of Maserfield in A.D. 642 and his dead body hanged, according to ancient tradition, from the gibbet at nearby Oswestry—'Oswald's tree'.

★   ★   ★

An important development in the work of the Corporation took place in 1874 when a public school for girls of the same social stratum as the boys provided for by its existing schools came into being at Abbots Bromley in Staffordshire. This was the outcome of the enthusiasm of Lowe, Provost of the Midland Division, aided and abetted by Henry Meynell, Vicar of Denstone, Sir Percival Heywood, and others who felt that at a time when public schools for girls were virtually non-existent a need and an opportunity presented themselves for the Church to undertake an entirely new pioneering enterprise in the field of education. One girls' school, at St Michael's, Bognor, affiliated to the Corporation as early as 1855, was incorporated in the Society in 1920. During the last war this school removed from Bognor and after a period of temporary sojourning migrated to its present home, Burton Park, near Petworth, where, in every respect a splendid example of a modern public school for girls, it continues to flourish and fully to justify its incorporation.

The Provost himself, however, had a curious prejudice against the girls' schools forming part of the Corporation, a prejudice which persisted with him until the close of his life; and although St Michael's, Bognor, and St Mary and St Anne's, Abbots Bromley, were followed, largely as a consequence of Lowe's untiring zeal, by the founding of St Winifred's at Bangor in 1887 (removing to Llanfairfechan in 1922), it was not until 1890, when Woodard was virtually on his death-bed, that these schools were brought into the full fellowship of the Society, and it was not until 1894, when the Founder's draft statutes were superseded by a formal constitution, that the various divisions were free to own and open schools for girls. Since that date, of course, several more have been founded or acquired; amongst them, Queen Margaret's at Scarborough (1901), Queen Ethelburga's at Harrogate (1912), Queen Mary's, Helmsley (1925), St Katherine's, Taunton (1919)[1] St Clare's, Penzance (1928) and St Hilary's, Alderley Edge, and these admirable academies occupy an important and esteemed position in the Corporation of St Mary and St Nicolas.

[1]For economic reasons, this school has since been closed.

Woodard had for some time been anxious to inaugurate a Western Division, and in 1879 his opportunity to do so materialized when the buildings and land of the Collegiate School, Taunton, came into the public market. This establishment, which traced its descent back to Tudor times, had fallen on somewhat difficult days. It had been built in 1523 by Bishop Fox of Winchester, founder of Corpus Christi College, Oxford, and was for long known as Bishop Fox's Grammar School. In the eighteenth century it was a flourishing provincial centre of learning with over two hundred pupils, but like so many of the ancient grammar schools it suffered a sharp decline in its fortunes in the course of the next hundred years or so. By the middle of the nineteenth century there were only twenty boys in the school. The situation was temporarily retrieved in 1867 when, by arrangement with the Charity Commissioners, a committee under the chairmanship of Lord Taunton took over the school which three years later they removed to a site outside the town, Bishop Fox's old buildings being sold to the municipality. The school, however, failed from a variety of reasons to flourish in its new surroundings, its financial position rapidly deteriorated and the land and buildings were heavily mortgaged. In 1879 the mortagees, anxious to realize what they could, put the property up to public auction with a reserve price on it of £12,500. There was, however, no bid and after a suitable pause Woodard, who had been closely watching development, privately offered £8,000 for the buildings, equipment and fourteen acres of land. This offer was eventually accepted, although the mortgage owners of the apparently unwanted property unreasonably complained that Woodard had been hard on them.

To stimulate local interest and enthusiasm a meeting was held in Taunton in April of the following year, with the Lord Lieutenant, the Earl of Cork, in the chair and the Bishop of the diocese, Beresford-Hope, M.P., Luttrell of Dunster, and the famous and fiery Archdeacon Denison on the platform. For the first time to a west of England audience, Woodard explained the principles of his foundations and insisted that the Church of England had a ministry of teaching which she had for long neglected. The newly-acquired school was formally dedicated in honour of King Alfred by the Bishop of Bath and Wells (Lord Arthur Harvey) on 26 October. The Bishop of Ely (J. R. Woodford) preached, and the choir of Ardingly College were brought down specially to sing at the service.

Woodard had hoped that Bishop Benson of Truro would accept the position of Provost of the new Western Division, but before that could be proposed Benson was translated to the Archbishopric of Canterbury. King's School, Taunton, remained, therefore, under Woodard's direct control until his death; but in 1897 a Western Division was formally brought into being, with a constitution similar to that of the Midlands and with a Provost and prominent men as Fellows. King's, Taunton, remains the only boys' school in the Division, though, as has already been mentioned, two girls' schools—St Katherine's, Heatherton Park, Taunton, and St Clare's, Penzance— were brought under its direction in 1919 and 1928 respectively.

*   *   *

The year 1887 saw the signal expression of the Church of England's official benediction upon all that Woodard had lived and laboured for when the Primate of all England, Archbishop Benson, consented to be present and preach at the dedication of Denstone College on 17 July. In his letter of acceptance to the Provost and Fellows of the Midland Division, His Grace wrote:

> The gratitude is great which the Church and Country owe to the Founder and his friends for the faith and perseverance with which they had conciliated so much devotion and affection to this great cause. I look forward to the fulfilling of your kind wish that I should be with you at the Dedication of the Chapel of St. Chad's College, Denstone.[1]

The Archbishop preached on the text: 'All things are yours: whether Paul, or Apollos, or Cephas, or the world, or life or death, or things present, or things to come'. The collection taken during the service amounted to the remarkable sum of £1,500

[1]Otter—p. 324.

and enabled the balance of the chapel's cost to be paid forthwith. Whatever the shortcomings of Victorian churchmen may
have been, meanness towards God was not one of them.
They gave of their abundance with a liberality which puts to
irredeemable shame the nicely-calculated less or more of much
that passes for almsgiving in our demonstrably less generous
age.

The process of the Corporation's expansion in the Midlands
was continued in that same year (1887) when the Duke of
Newcastle offered, and Woodard accepted, a site of 100 acres
for a new school between the Nottinghamshire mining town of
Worksop and the ducal seat of Clumber. The foundation stone
of this latest addition to the Society's schools was laid by the
duke on 4 September 1890, in the presence of a large concourse
including representatives from all the other schools. One
familiar face, however, was missing. Woodard himself was
too ill to be present. The Father Founder was approaching
the end of his earthly pilgrimage and early in July he had
appointed three commissioners, of whom his son William was
one, to exercise the functions of Provost should he become
physically or mentally incapacitated. There is no evidence that
they ever exercised independently that delegated authority,
though during the last months of Woodard's life they undoubtedly acted for him on his instructions in many important
matters connected with the Society. As to Worksop, it remains
to be recorded that the college, dedicated to St Cuthbert, was
opened in 1895, and that the magnificent chapel, the gift of
Lord Mountgarret, was designed by the distinguished architect,
Sir Aston Webb. Worksop, being the latest of the boys' schools,
is also the most up-to-date and since its foundation many new
buildings and extensions have put it into the forefront of
modern public schools.

★   ★   ★

Woodard was essentially a home-loving man and can scarcely
have enjoyed his periods of official residence in Manchester,
where he lived on his own in lodgings. It was always a tremendous relief to him to return home to the circle of his loved ones,

amongst whom he was invariably in the highest spirits at the
end of the day's work, however wearisome or discouraging it
might have been. In the intimate circle of his family and friends
he seldom found it difficult to relax, to cast off the cares which
beset so many of his days and frequently to indulge in the most
hilarious diversions. It was probably this ability to shed for a
space the problems and worries attaching to his work which
enabled him to bear so indefatigably and for so long the
immense burden of responsibility which devolved upon him
from the inception of his scheme.

Of the inner life of the soul which above all sustained him he
was not accustomed to say much, but in a letter to Lowe, dated
22 October 1886, he wrote:

> The most painful moments of my life are the two hours before
> rising in the morning, when I have to say the Lord's Prayer with
> all its petitions enlarged and dwelt upon, for all the wants of the
> day.
>
> As a custodian of a work of singular moment to the Country,
> and which God has evidently entrusted to me, I move with great
> fear and I pray daily that neither the love for pleasing others, or
> [sic] a narrow and ignorant and vain prejudice may injuriously
> influence my acts.

The sentiments expressed in this letter reveal the Provost—
not, indeed, as in any way a mystic or contemplative; he was
ever the man of action and affairs—but most unmistakably as a
man of prayer and spirituality, as one possessed of a consuming
sense of particular vocation superimposed upon his priestly
calling. Therein, supremely, lay the secret of his great strength.

For a considerable part of his active life Woodard was to find
himself misrepresented and misunderstood over the question
which used to be, and perhaps still is—with the possible exception of the use of incense in church—the Englishman's greatest
religious bugbear, sacramental confession and priestly absolution. Although in this matter the Provost's position was always
strictly that of the Book of Common Prayer, from the time of his
prolonged passage of arms with Bishop Blomfield of London he
was constantly under fire—mostly from Protestant quarters,
since it was charged with tedious reiteration that the St Nicolas'

schools were forcing houses of Romanism—but also at times from the more extreme Anglo-Catholic wing, which accused him of temporizing and timidity. Anyone who is so simultaneously attacked from such diametrically opposed extremes may, per-haps, reasonably feel reassured as to the essential soundness of his position, and Woodard indeed was at all times meticulously careful in seeing to it that what was taught and practised in the schools of his foundation was in strict accord and harmony with Anglican principles. Confession was at no time and in no respect compulsory, nor was it ever made the condition for the receiving of any other sacrament or spiritual privilege. The 'How' and 'Why' of making confession before a priest, and the grace available through the channel of sacramental absolution, were carefully explained to each candidate as a constituent part of his preparation for Confirmation, while the majority of the confessions made, besides being entirely voluntary, were and are preparatory to the receiving of that rite.

Woodard regarded his schools as schools for the spiritual, mental and physical nourishment of the sons (and later, daughters) of the Church, of all parties and none. The standard of churchmanship in each of these schools must be that of the Church of England as enshrined in her Prayer Book and Canon Law. Confession before a priest is not only permitted by the Book of Common Prayer, but in certain circumstances enjoined (though never demanded); so it must be in the schools of the Woodard Corporation. Similarly the Prayer Book provides for the use of the Eucharistic vestments and plainly upholds the Holy Communion service as the principal act of Anglican Sunday worship. In requiring that the Holy Eucharist shall be celebrated every Sunday and Holy Day in all their school chapels the statutes of the Society of St Nicolas and St Mary are framed in obedience to and in conformity with the *lex orandi* of the Church of England, and they ensure the maintenance of that position adopted from the first in these matters by the Founder himself.

Beyond the Church's requirements in these things Woodard rigidly refused to go but, equally firmly, he would have nothing to do with a standard of observance which in any respect fell short of them. It is because of his unswerving adherence to Anglican liturgical and doctrinal standards that the worship and teaching to be found in the chapel of any school belonging to the Society constitute, within human limits, the perfect expression of what Anglican worship and Anglican teaching ought everywhere to be. It is neither 'High', 'Low', 'Broad' nor 'Great Central'; it is neither Anglo-Catholic, Protestant nor Modernist. It is Prayer Book Churchmanship pure and simple, in which all who proclaim themselves loyal members of the Church of England may, if they will, find themselves at home in their Father's House.

In spite of persistent pleadings on the part of many of his friends, Woodard steadfastly refused to have his portrait painted. He protested that such an action would be widely misunderstood and misinterpreted as an attempt to draw attention to himself and a stressing of his own personal achievements to the exclusion, or at least the belittling, of the sacrifices, benefactions and efforts of those who had been associated with him in his life-work. Nor would he consent to be photographed, though on the occasion of the conferring of his doctor's degree at Oxford he was somehow or other lured into it, and from the photograph taken then a portrait was later painted and hung in the Hall at Lancing. To many people today, hardened and accustomed as they are to publicity, boosting and ballyhoo on behalf of anyone who has achieved even the moderately unusual, Woodard's reluctance in this respect to accede to his friends' very understandable wish for some enduring likeness of the man they loved and admired may appear excessive and perhaps unnatural. Yet it is truly indicative of the character of the man who, for all his autocratic temper and instinct for keeping so far as practicable the strings of control in his own hands, was essentially humble and lowly of heart. He was perfectly capable of assessing his own capacities while in all things attributing the glory to God, but self-aggrandizement occupied no place in his plans and purpose.

*   *   *

Since October 1862, when he had removed from Shoreham, Woodard lived at Martin Lodge at Henfield in Sussex, a spacious house with attractive grounds and gardens. Here he delighted to dispense hospitality at all times and to all and sundry, while each Christmas the communicants of the parish were entertained at a party where he not only proved himself the perfect host but also brewed for his guests the perfect hot punch. His wife, the loyal, unobtrusive, devoted partner of his life from those early days of studious drudgery and plain living in Oxford, died in 1873. From thenceforth, until her marriage to Sir John Otter, his one daughter, Elizabeth Audrey, kept house for him and acted as hostess to his numerous and frequently distinguished guests. In the year before he died Woodard married Miss Dorothy Porritt. The death of his eldest son, Mortimer, in the early part of 1888, had cast its sombre shadows over the closing years of the Provost's life and probably hastened the final breakdown of his physical powers, worn and weakened as they must already have been by years of unrelenting toil and anxiety.

Woodard died on St Mark's Day, 25 April 1891, in his eighty-first year, and was buried in a vault beside the crypt of the chapel at Lancing. He is commemorated in the chapel itself by a chantry designed by G. Temple Moore, with an effigy in bronze by P. Bryant Baker. This effigy and the portrait in the hall are the only existing likenesses of the Founder, all that we have to record for us what manner of man he was in appearance and expression.

I cannot do better than quote the late Bishop of Oxford's description of these portraits, in *The Story of the Woodard Schools*.

He is shown as a man of delicately sensitive appearance; with thoughtful and almost dreamy eyes and a determined chin. There is a hint at the corner of the lips and eyes alike of that whimsical sense of humour which (so those who knew him say) often made him a delightfully boyish companion. The forehead is massive; and although the face is in complete repose, the repose is that of a powerful will waiting for the moment when it shall be summoned to activity. He seems in the painting, to be listening to an argument from some member of his Chapter; weighing it up impersonally, estimating its strength and its weaknesses, carrying it forward along different lines of conjecture towards results of which its author is unconscious; and all the time holding in reserve his own firm standards, against which to test it when its own intrinsic worth has been elicited. There is no trace of bigotry in the face; but it indicates a wealth of hidden enthusiasm and an unswerving attachment to principle. Above all, it is a very peaceful face; and perhaps that gives the secret of Woodard's greatness.[1]

'The secret of Woodard's greatness.' The quality of greatness is frequently easier to recognize than to analyse. In assessing, or attempting to assess, what constitutes it in particular instances from past generations we can turn only to the judgement of contemporaries and to recorded achievements. Sufficient tributes from the men of his own generation have already been quoted to establish Woodard's claim to veneration in the eyes of his own contemporaries. As to his achievement eight flourishing public schools for boys brought under the *aegis* of his Society within his own lifetime, as well as an equal number of successful schools for girls founded or acquired before or since his death, constitute in themselves an indisputable testimony to his vision, energy and enthusiasm as well as to his vast administrative and organizing powers.

As a founder of Christian schools Woodard was in the direct line of succession from Alfred, Alcuin, William of Wykeham, Henry VI, William Waynflete, Richard Fox, John Colet and Thomas Bray; but it is not in the number of his foundations that he claims the reverence of posterity so much as in the nature of them. The Woodard schools occupy splendid sites and boast many noble buildings, but the heart and centre of their daily life and work is in the school chapel which the Founder always insisted should be centrally situated and nobly planned. The schools can look back with pride upon the first-rate scholars and athletes, the distinguished men and women in many varied walks of life whom they have produced. But their greatest achievement, their deepest claim upon the affection, admiration and gratitude of all who set store by the things of the spirit, rests upon the many thousands now who, as boys and girls from the homes of the numerous and influential English middle class,

[1]Kirk—pp. 44–45.

learnt between their walls and beneath their sheltering roofs what is good and what the Lord required of them; to do justly, to love mercy, and to walk humbly with their God. From the chapels of the Woodard schools, fortified through the laying-on of hands and strengthened with the Bread of Life, those boys and girls have gone out to play their part in the life of Church and State and, by God's grace, to contribute their leaven to the surrounding worldly lump.

To this end Nathaniel Woodard worked and prayed and pleaded and lived his laborious days. To this end the generous-minded laity of his era gave of their munificence and liberality. To this end the schools of the Corporation of SS. Mary and Nicolas continue the God-inspired work of their Founder, to whom the Anglican Church owes a debt incalculable because it cannot be reckoned in terms of cash or lands or bricks and mortar.

Herein, surely, lies the true claim to greatness, and to the undying gratitude of his fellow churchmen and women, of the modest country curate who saw visions and dreamed dreams to which he gave noble habitations and an imperishable name; who, after he had in his own generation served God so faithfully, fell on sleep and was laid unto his fathers.

CHAPTER VI

CROWN FOR THE VALIANT

T HE Victorian era was an age of abundance and expansion in many departments of life. It was a period of tremendous activity in Church life and affairs; a period of revival, restoration and innovation. A rapidly increasing population called for increased accommodation in parish churches—a demand which, not always adequately met at the time, declined rapidly during the first half of the present century. The work of the Oxford Movement in proclaiming the spiritual authority and mission of the Church resulted inevitably in a widespread improvement in the standards of public worship and a demand for greater warmth, dignity and beauty in the services of the Church. The altar successfully challenged the pulpit for the place of pre-eminence; its ornaments and those of the ministers who officiated at it were restored in accordance with what the protagonists of the Movement deemed to be the correct interpretation of the famous 'Ornaments Rubric' of the Book of Common Prayer.

Music began to play an ever-increasing part in public worship, and particularly did this become the case in the matter of hymns and hymn-singing. Verses set to music had always formed an important element in Christian worship. The Jewish Psalter provided an obvious source from the beginning of the Church's history, but this was soon supplemented by compositions from Christian pens. The Syriac, Greek and Latin service books of the first ten centuries contain a rich store of compilations. In England, from the time of Caedmon down to the Reformation, vernacular hymns, many of them translations from the Latin, were popular and numerous. At the Reformation, while Lutheranism made great use of new hymns, many of them written by Martin Luther himself, the Calvinists would tolerate nothing in their worship other than the actual words of Scripture. Hence the metrical versions of the Psalms still in use in Calvinistic worship such as that of the Church of Scotland. In England, likewise, hymns found no place in the Book of Common Prayer,[1] but this was probably due to Cranmer's literary gifts and inclinations tending rather towards prose than to poetry. There were, however, English metrical versions of the Psalter from the sixteenth century to the nineteenth, the best known being those of Sternhold and Hopkins which appeared in 1557, and of Tate and Brady, which came out in 1696.

In the eighteenth century hymn writing and hymn singing received a great impetus from the Methodist and Evangelical Movements, the great names being those of Isaac Watts, John and Charles Wesley (the latter the most prolific of all English hymnographers), P. Doddridge, John Newton, William Cowper and A. Toplady. These writers produced for the most part hymns of an emotional and subjective nature, and in an age which looked askance at anything in the nature of religious 'enthusiasm', hymn-singing tended to be regarded with considerable distrust and distaste by the authorities of the Church, as well as by worshippers in general. Nevertheless, Reginald Heber, a Shropshire clergyman who later became Bishop of Calcutta, both wrote and collected a number of original hymns, which were published in 1827, a year after his death. This work, *Hymns written and Adapted to the Weekly Church Services of the Year*, did a great deal to overcome the popular prejudice against hymns, and so did such famous by-products of the Oxford Movement as Keble's *Christian Year* and J. H. Newman's *Dream of Gerontius*. By the middle of the nineteenth century, hymn singing was firmly established as an important element in the public worship of the Church of England, and the way was open for the publication of such collections as *The Hymnal Noted* (1852–54), *Hymns Ancient and Modern* (1861), *The English Hymnal* (1906) and *Songs of Praise* (1925).

[1]With the one exception of the *Veni Creator* in the Ordinal.

Most of these hymnaries contain a considerable number of ancient hymns translated from Greek or, more usually, Latin originals; and of these translations a great many are the work of a man who was typically Victorian in the prodigious amount of literary achievement which he contrived to pack into a lifetime of less than fifty years—a lifetime incidentally dogged by persistent poor health and frequent persecution.

*   *   *

John Mason Neale was born in London, in Lamb's Conduit Street, on 24 January 1818. He came of a sternly evangelical stock, and his early and formative years were overshadowed by the death of his father when he himself was only 5 years old. Thereafter his religious upbringing was mainly in the hands of his mother and followed closely the accepted pattern of an evangelical household of the time. He was brought up to know and love the stories and characters of the Bible, to fear God, and to observe a moral code of the most uncompromising kind. Twice a Sunday he was taken to hear sermons of what would nowadays be regarded as inordinate length, the texts of which he was required carefully to take note of and to memorize. To help fill in the long and perilous period between morning and evening service, Mrs Neale would read aloud in the course of the afternoon one or more of Dr Doddridge's sermons.

This formidable spiritual diet, which in these enlightened days of widespread juvenile delinquency would be held account-able for all manner of repressions, complexes and psychopathic abnormalities, does not appear to have had any unduly adverse effects upon the fatherless boy. He seems to have enjoyed a normal, happy boyhood, first at the peaceful riverside village of Chiswick, and then at the even more remote and rural river-side hamlet of Shepperton. Original Sin at times successfully resisted the totalitarian onslaughts of Sabbatarianism; his old nurse could describe him with deep affection as 'the dearest, dirtiest, lyingest boy' she had ever known. Fairy tales may have played little part in lightening his leisure hours, but from an early age his imaginative and historical senses were highly developed and he began to move familiarly in golden realms of bygone romance and mystic wonder.

'About a mile and a half from here,' he says in a letter written before he was 10 years old, 'is a great cavern which you pay sixpence a-piece for seeing, where Jack Cade, who lived in the reign of Henry VI, and a great many robbers have kept their spoils.'

Happy the growing boy for whom the glamour of the past can suffuse the shades of the prison house. The Vision Splendid is reflected at least as frequently in the pages of history as in the often murky records of current affairs.

From the age of 11 until he was 15, Neale attended a private school at Blackheath. From thence he went for two years to Sherborne, where he seems not to have distinguished himself to any marked degree, beyond demonstrating an utter inaptitude for athletic pursuits.

At Trinity College, Cambridge, whither he went up in 1836, he found himself in surroundings frequented not so long since by such figures of subsequent literary eminence as Tennyson, Thackeray, Arthur Hallam, James Spedding of Mirehouse and Edward Fitzgerald. More significantly, he was simultaneously caught up in the exhilarating stream of ideas set in motion by the Oxford Tractarians, and in the equally exciting discovery, to him, of the theological and liturgical treasures of the Early Church. The Latin poets of the Middle Ages also presented themselves to his notice, but his first published work in this field was the translation of a commentary from St Bernard on Psalm XCI. This led the way to subsequent translations of hymns from the Roman and Gallican breviaries.

Of almost equal importance was the beginning, during his Cambridge days, of a life-long friendship with Benjamin Webb, a fellow undergraduate and fellow enthusiast for all that is embraced by the term 'ecclesiology'—early Christian art, architecture, ancient manuscripts, religious symbolism and hymnology. Together they founded, in May 1839, the Cambridge Camden Society for promoting and encouraging the study of these interests, the Society's first president being T. Thorp, Archdeacon of Bristol and Fellow and Tutor of Trinity.

Among the early members were Harvey Goodwin, afterwards Bishop of Carlisle, F. A. Paley, Augustus Pugin, Edward
Boyce and Edmund Venables. So rapidly did the Society ex-
pand that before it had been in existence for five years it could
already boast, as patrons or members, two archbishops, sixteen
bishops, twenty-one archdeacons, thirty-one peers and members of parliament, sixteen leading architects and over seven
hundred ordinary members—a remarkable achievement on the
part of two not otherwise eminent undergraduates. In 1841 the
Society began to publish a monthly periodical, *The Ecclesiologist*,
as well as papers read to gatherings of its members. Among the
latter was one by Neale on 'Ecclesiastical Monumental Brasses'.
In 1846 the headquarters of the Cambridge Camden Society
were removed to London, and thereafter it became officially
known as the 'Ecclesiological Society', surviving as such until
1863. Through its meetings, publications and other activities,
the Society was instrumental in arousing widespread interest in
ecclesiastical art and architecture, and in assisting to a signifi-
cant degree the subsequent liturgical and ceremonial revival.

After a short period as chaplain and tutor at Downing
College, Neale was ordained deacon in St Margaret's Church,
Westminster, by the Bishop of Gloucester, on Trinity Sunday,
6 June 1841, and he preached his first sermon in the village
church in Shepperton, where a considerable part of his boyhood
had been spent. In the following autumn he resigned his chap-
laincy of Downing, and began parochial work as assistant curate
in the parish of St Nicolas, Guildford. His stay in this parish
proved to be of brief duration. Bishop Sumner of Winchester
found himself unable to license in his diocese an originator of
the notorious Camden Society, so Neale was compelled to
relinquish his appointment and return to Cambridge. During
the period which followed he published the first of his historical
stories for young people—*Herbert Tresham, a Story of the Great
Rebellion*. Such works of fiction, agreeably inculcating moral
purpose or useful knowledge, enjoyed considerable popularity
in the nineteenth century, and Neale employed his versatile pen
on several of them in order to propagate among the rising
generation the ideas behind the current Church revival.

Ordained priest on Trinity Sunday, 1842, Neale was next day offered and accepted the benefice of Crawley in Sussex, at that time a small village with few inhabitants. This was to be his first and last parochial charge, but in spite of his youth and inexperience (for he was only twenty-four), and in spite of being plunged from the companionship and intellectual stimulus of university life into the stolid rusticity of rural Sussex, Neale seems to have adapted himself to his new surroundings with surprising facility. Nor did his 'advanced' doctrines and liturgical observances apparently do more than mildly surprise his unprogressive flock. No doubt, as country folk have a habit of doing, they listened patiently to all that he had to say and teach, and then proceeded placidly upon their accustomed ways of devotion and observance. 'Silly Sussex won't be druv' and is uncommonly hard to lead. All it normally asks is to be left alone to practise its easy-going, unadventurous, conventional churchmanship in its own contented time-honoured way. It is not magnificent but it is rural religion—in no wise peculiar to the county of Sussex, but easily to be paralleled in any of her thirty-nine sister shires. It has broken the heart of many a zealous priest on fire with enthusiasm for the Catholic Faith and the Kingdom of God. It has provided a cast-iron defence for many a country incumbent, settled comfortably on his lees and ever ready to plead in extenuation of the state of virtual spiritual stagnation existing in his parish, 'My people love to have it so.'

Neale, however, was not destined to break his heart in the village of Crawley, still less to sink into any unresisting acquiescence with things as they were. His health, which had never been robust, now began to deteriorate rapidly. He began to suffer from fever and from pains in the chest. Medical opinion was sought and a change of environment was decreed. After only a few weeks as incumbent of Crawley he was compelled to resign the benefice. It was during this crisis in his physical and vocational affairs that he decided the time was ripe for him to marry.

His enforced retirement from parochial work provided Neale with ample leisure for literary pursuits, and during the following months he occupied himself with the production of such varied works as *Hymns for the Sick, Songs and Ballads for the People, Hierologus, or the Church Tourists, Ayton Priory,* and *Symbolism of Churches: translated from the First Book of Durandus*—the latter a piece of work done in conjunction with Webb. As his health continued to be unsatisfactory, he began to reconcile himself to a more or less permanent exclusion from parochial activity, but his literary output continued unabated. *Hymns for Children, Agnes de Tracy: a Tale of the Times of S. Thomas of Canterbury, Letter on Private Devotion in Churches, Songs and Ballads for Manufacturers,* followed one another in rapid succession.

The malady which afflicted his lungs in no way reduced his muscular powers, and he was able to take long walks on summer days, visiting churches and other buildings of historical and architectural interest over a wide area of the county. The winters, however, he found excessively trying, and he soon felt it necessary to migrate each autumn to milder climes—first to Penzance in Cornwall and then, for three successive winters, to Madeira. It was in this island that he made the acquaintance of the famous French historian Charles Montalembert, the associate in the movement towards a more liberal Catholicism of Pères Lammenais and Lacordaire. The two men found many common interests and had numerous conversations on ecclesiastical affairs. The Frenchman was generous in his praise and encouragement of Neale's historical work, but entirely failed to convince the younger man that the Anglican Church was heretical and schismatic. This inevitable divergence on the point which still divides Romanist and Anglican was not allowed to impair the personal friendship between two men of such similar tastes and interests, so fortuitously brought together far from their respective homelands. Neale, with his great enthusiasm for Primitive Christianity, and with his admiration for the Eastern Churches where he felt that the ideal had been most purely preserved, could never admit the totalitarian claims of the Papacy to be valid. In a letter to Webb about this time we find him writing:

> Without becoming a shade more Anglican, I do see more and more clearly that the High Papal theory is quite untenable. . . . I cannot make, as Montalembert does, or as the C. sometimes

seemed to wish to do, the desire for visible union with the Chair of St. Peter, the Keystone as it were of the Church—at least, not in the sense in which the Western Church has sometimes done. *We Orientals* take a more general view. The Rock upon which the Church is built is St. Peter, but it is a triple Rock: Antioch where he sat, Alexandria which he superintended, Rome where he suffered. You would be astonished at the weight of evidence in Doctors of the Western Church.

★　　★　　★

From his earlier studies in Byzantine art and Oriental languages, Neale had acquired a deep veneration for the Orthodox Churches of the East, and early in 1843 he had begun to formulate a new literary project inspired by this enthusiasm. He had written to Webb: 'I think I might undertake a very favourite plan of mine; a history of the Eastern Church to the present time—perhaps only from the great schism of East and West.' This massive work was begun in 1843, during his exile in Madeira. It involved a tremendous amount of research and poring over ancient documents—decrees of councils, martyrologies, histories, liturgies, sermons, and theological writings of the Greek and Latin Fathers, as well as of medieval and more modern writings throwing light on his tremendous theme. He was aided in his work by his own astonishing linguistic ability; he knew some twenty languages—an invaluable gift when it came to dealing with original documents. The completed work —*The History of the Holy Eastern Church*—occupied him over most of his lifetime. *The History of Alexandria* (two volumes) was published in 1847, and the *Introduction*, held back in order that valuable information might be obtained from Constantinople, was published (also in two volumes) in 1850. The final volume, on *The Patriarchate of Antioch*, was unfinished at his death. It was completed by the Reverend George Williams and appeared in 1878.

Neale returned to England in 1845 to find a state of great excitement and uncertainty prevailing in Church circles everywhere as a consequence of Newman's secession to Rome. Many more disciples of the Tractarian leader were soon to follow his example—Faber, Oakley, and Dalgairns among them. The hearts of many who remained loyal were heavy with foreboding for the future of Catholic principles and ideals in the Anglican communion, but Neale does not appear to have shared the encircling gloom. Like Keble, Pusey, Liddon, Church and many others, he not only remained steadfast in his allegiance, but contemplated the future with faith and hope if not with immoderate optimism. The secessions had upon him the bracing effect of a spiritual 'Dunkirk' and, having survived what so many had feared might prove the fatal worst, the future he felt could now be faced with calmness and a reasonable measure of confidence.

In November 1845 Neale won the prize awarded annually, under the bequest of the Reverend Thomas Seaton of Clare College, Cambridge, for the best English poem on a sacred subject, and £20 of the award he gave towards the building of a church at Farncombe, near Godalming, where his friend, E. J. Boyce, was vicar. Altogether, Neale won the 'Seatonian' eleven years in succession.

★   ★   ★

In 1846 the Wardenship of Sackville College, at East Grinstead, in Sussex, fell vacant and the post was offered to Neale. The College had been founded in 1608 by Robert, second Earl of Dorset, for the shelter and maintenance of thirty poor and aged householders. It was under the rule of a warden, who was provided with a house within the college and a stipend of £28 a year. There was a chapel and refectory but these, like most of the college buildings, were in a state of considerable disrepair. Neither the condition of the College nor the emoluments of the wardenship offered any great attractions. The appointment was not likely to lead to further preferment, the obligation of publicly reciting the Offices in chapel were a virtual tie so far as the warden was concerned, and it offered its holder little in the way of scope for pastoral or prophetic ministrations. Nevertheless, such a situation had its appeal for one more concerned with literary output than with ecclesiastical advancement, and when the appointment was offered to Neale he had no hesitation in accepting. He took up residence at the College on 26 May 1846, and there he was destined to continue for the remaining twenty years of his life.

The time-weathered buildings, with their vine and rose-covered walls surrounding a mellowed quadrangle of close-cut velvety lawns presented, for all their dilapidated inward state, an agreeable aspect of refuge and repose for its aged occupants and their comparatively youthful warden. The deep central porch was flanked by oaken benches where the old people could sit and sun themselves of a summer's day, as their predecessors had done for over two centuries; the heavy oak door, with its date, 1616, and the sundial above the southern porch bearing the inscription *Horas non numero nisi serenas*, each testified to a slumbrous, ancient peace disturbed but seldom over the passing years. Now, through the generous assistance of the De la Warr family, heirs of the Dorset estates and patrons of the College, repairs to the buildings were speedily put in hand. The hall was restored, the great fireplace, long disused, was opened out, and rooms hitherto unoccupied through disrepair were put in order for the accommodation of a greater number of homeless and indigent pensioners.

But it was not only in restoring the buildings that Neale's reforming zeal found an outlet. He soon discovered that many of the College's ancient statutes had come to be quietly disregarded, notably those which required the Warden and inmates to meet in chapel, morning and evening, 'there to pray, serve, honour and praise Almighty God'. The daily services were held from the beginning of Neale's wardenship, and the old people were urged and encouraged to attend them in obedience to the Founder's desires. At the Sunday services his simple, homely talks brought new light to his hearers or rekindled forgotten truths. Disturbed from the placid, uninspiring routine of their daily existence, the aged Collegians came to appreciate the zeal and sincerity which lay behind Neale's insistence upon attendance in chapel, as well as his loving concern for their entire welfare—spiritual as well as material. His own house and table were open to them on occasion, while on Sundays and Saints' days it was his custom to dine with them in

hall—the young father at the head of his family table. Sometimes he would send for certain of the poorer villagers to join
them in the plain but plentiful fare provided.

One of his earliest concerns, as became a co-founder of the
Cambridge Camden Society, was the restoration and beautify-
ing of the College chapel. An oak belfry was erected and three
bells hung therein; open benches replaced the tall old box
pews; the altar was vested with the customary ornaments and
the great rood over the chancel arch set up.

For a time things went on peacefully at the College, the
warden busily occupied in improving its interior arrangements
and administration; the pensioners happy under the care of
one who, though his years were few compared with their own,
was clearly so liberally endowed with learning, love and concern for their well-being.

This happy state of things, however, was destined not to
endure. These were times of religious tension, suspicion and
high party feeling. In the eyes of the average Englishman Rome
was still something to be feared and consequently hated, as
much from political as from religious motives. Catholic Emanci-
pation and the subsequent progress made by Roman Catholic
missions in Britain had done nothing to diminish the fears or
the antagonism, to which fresh force was imparted by the
secession of Newman and his disciples. The Oxford Movement,
the *Tracts for the Times*, together with all outward manifestations
of the Catholic Revival in the Church of England of a ceremonial or liturgical character, were popularly condemned as
part of a conspiracy to betray the principles of the Reformation
and to bring Englishmen once more under papal domination.
In London and other large centres of population, where
devoted priests were labouring heroically amongst the poor and
the underprivileged, organized mobs of hooligans were set on
to riot and demonstrate in the sacred cause of 'No Popery!'
Protestant fanaticism in all its ugliest guises was fanned into
flame from its ever-smouldering embers; the ignorant, the
brutal and the depraved providing a ready instrument in the
hands of unscrupulous partisans.

Remote though it then was, Sackville College was not to be

left undisturbed by this recrudescence of religious bigotry. A certain Mr Hutton, who had come to live in the vicinity though not in the parish nor even in the diocese, called at the College and was received with every courtesy by the warden. Having been shown all there was to see, Hutton then announced that the purpose of his visit was to look for suspected innovations in the way of ornament or ceremony and to report any such to the Bishop of Chichester. This amiable intention he proceeded to put into effect, informing his Lordship that in the College chapel he had discovered a copy of the Vulgate version of the Bible and a Roman breviary. The Bishop was suitably horrified, but since the College was extra-diocesan and not under his episcopal jurisdiction he brought the complaint to the notice of the patron, Earl De la Warr, who at once communicated the matter to Neale.

The latter made it perfectly clear that both the Book of Common Prayer, and the Authorized Version of the Bible were used, and none other, for the services held in the College chapel, and that the books complained of were his own private property, principally used in connexion with his historical and liturgical studies. This explanation Lord De la Warr found completely satisfying, but not so Bishop Gilbert who, after inconclusive correspondence and a personal visit to the College, inhibited Neale from the exercise of his priestly functions anywhere in the diocese of Chichester.[1] In a further letter, emphasizing his disapproval of what he termed the unspiritual adjuncts of worship which the Warden had introduced into the chapel—very modest and harmless additions by present-day standards—the Bishop permitted himself to refer immoderately to Neale's attempts 'to debase the minds of these poor people with his spiritual haberdashery'.

Disregarding the appeals against his decision made by Neale himself, by Lord De la Warr and by the pensioners of the College, Bishop Gilbert remained adamant. The pensioners were curtly told that their warden must have 'perplexed their minds with new and strange shows and observances', and that he

[1]Except, of course, in the Chapel of Sackville College, over which the Bishop had no jurisdiction.

could not alter his decision. The ban was, in fact, to remain in force for sixteen years, only being finally removed in November 1863, three years before Neale's death.

★   ★   ★

From this unhappy episode, so discreditable to those responsible and doubly distressing to a man of deep sensitivity, Neale sought and found distraction in fresh application to his literary projects. His study became at once the scene of his most onerous labours and a haven from the storms of ecclesiastical controversy. Here, between shelves crammed with manuscripts and books of every kind, architectural and ecclesiological treatises, volumes of the works of the Early Christian Fathers of East and West, folklore, hymnology, grammars and dictionaries representing every European and a great many Oriental languages, Neale undoubtedly passed his happiest hours.

He now resumed, as his principal task, his monumental *History of the Eastern Church*, the two volumes of the *History of Alexandria* duly appearing in print early in 1847. At the same time, and largely no doubt by way of relaxation, he occupied himself with writing of a still serious though probably less exacting kind—stories for children, liturgical studies, a commentary on the Psalms, hymnological writings and sundry translations issuing in an unending stream from his prolific pen. His mental and literary assiduity were matched only by his astonishing versatility but, as though in refutation of the belief that a Jack-of-all-trades can be master of none, his deepest researches and most constant application were devoted to his *magnum opus* on the Oriental Churches.

In this work Neale found the fullest scope for his instinctive scholarship, the most satisfying object for his generous enthusiasm. Here at times he is constrained to throw aside the customary restraint of the scholar and the historian, as in the eloquent tribute to the Eastern Church which appears in the opening pages of his 'Introduction'.

In the glow and splendour of the Byzantine glory, in the tempest of the Oriental Middle Ages, in the desolation and

tyranny of the Turkish Empire, the testimony of the same im-
mutable Church remains unchanged. Extending herself from the
sea of Okhotsk to the palaces of Venice, from the icefields which
grind against the Solevetsky monastery to the burning jungles of
the Malabar, embracing a thousand languages, nations and
tongues, but binding them together in the golden link of the same
faith; offering the tremendous Sacrifice in a hundred liturgies,
but offering it to the same God and with the same rites; fixing
her patriarchal thrones in the same cities as when the disciples
were called Christians first at Antioch, and James the brother of
the Lord finished his course at Jerusalem; oppressed by the
devotees of the False Prophet, as once by the worshippers of false
gods,—she is now, as she was from the beginning, multiplex in
her arrangements, simple in her faith, difficult of comprehension
to strangers, easily intelligible to her sons, widely scattered in her
branches, hardly beset by her enemies, yet still and evermore,
what she delights to call herself, One, Only, Holy, Catholic and
Apostolic. . . . For eighteen hundred years this venerable
Communion has fought the good fight and borne about in her
body the marks of the Lord Jesus. Since she armed Athanasius
against Arius and sent forth Cyril against Nestorius, unnumbered
heresies have assailed her . . . her existence itself has often-
times been a very agony, yet the gates of hell have never prevailed against her. Idolatry and Apostasy have attempted her
subjugation, and confessed her invincible; kings and caliphs,
emperors and sultans, have stood up against her, but the King of
kings and Lord of lords has been on her side. . . . In the great
regeneration of the Church, in the second and more blessed
Pentecost, the Ecumenical Throne of the East will bear no
small part.

Neale was inspired in his work on the Eastern Churches not
only by his profound interest in the subject itself, but also by a
burning desire for the reunion of divided Christendom. Among
the many barriers to this he recognized that the Anglican
ignorance of Orthodoxy and Orthodox ignorance of the
Anglican communion were not the least in importance. It was
in an endeavour to dispel at least some of this ignorance on the
part of his fellow Anglicans that Neale undertook his great
task. Although uncompleted in his own lifetime, his work did
not fail to find recognition among those best qualified to

appreciate its quality and underlying purpose. After the publication of the first two volumes Webb wrote to their author:

> Dr Pusey spent a long time with us most pleasantly. I showed him your book, which he looked over with great interest, and expressed a great joy that you had devoted yourself to anything so solid and valuable. He said we wanted nothing more than ecclesiastical history done by our own Church. He himself is full of schemes and devotion and energy.

About this time (1847–8) Neale made the acquaintance of the Reverend Eugene Popoff, chaplain at the Russian Embassy in London. Much correspondence between the two men on sundry aspects of Orthodox life and worship led to a deep and lasting friendship. When in London Neale frequently attended services at the Russian Embassy chapel. Through Popoff his work became known in Russian and Greek Church circles, and much valuable information came to him from these sources. He began to learn Russian Slavonic largely in order that he might make a translation of his *History* in that language, and he sought and obtained permission to dedicate the translation to the Czar.

From Smyrna came a letter of warm commendation from the Russian theologian Mouravieff of his *History of Alexandria*, offering his:

> plus sincéres remerciments pour le don précieux. Il m'a été aussi bien doux de voir l'esprit vraiment orthodox d'Orient qui régne dans toute l'ouvrage, comme s'il était écrit par un Catholique de'Orient. Votre exposition du Patriarchat de Cyrille Lucar est magnifique, et c'est vraiment un service rendu à l'Eglise d'Orient.

Even more distinguished recognition was to follow. On 10 June 1851, Popoff wrote to Neale:

> His Excellency our Ambassador, Baron de Brunnow, has kindly charged me to announce to you, that His Majesty the Emperor of Russia, in acknowledgment of the value of your arduous and useful work on 'The History of the Holy Eastern Church', as well as an encouragement of its continuance, has been graciously pleased to grant you the sum of £100.

However little honour the prophet, the poet and the scribe might enjoy in his own country and diocese, it must have been to him a matter of great encouragement and consolation to receive this generous and tangible tribute to his work from the Head of the then greatest of all Orthodox States.

*   *   *

The publication, early in 1850, of the Privy Council's judgement in the Gorham case aroused widespread indignation amongst Churchmen, and Neale was constrained to plunge into the ensuing fray with a pamphlet attacking the Erastian theory which lay behind the Council's assumption of ecclesiastical and doctrinal authority and defending the challenged teaching of Baptismal Regeneration. In support of his arguments Neale characteristically summoned as witnesses St Cyril, the opponent of the Nestorian heresy, and other Fathers of the Primitive Church, rather than more modern and possibly more controversial authorities. The pamphlet was published in Lent of that year (1850) and brought Neale many expressions of support and gratitude from all over the country, notably a letter of profound thanks from the Reverend W. J. E. Bennett who invited him to preach one of the sermons during the octave of the consecration of St Barnabas, Pimlico. This sermon was afterwards published under the title of *The Church's Extremity, God's Opportunity*.

Not long after the publication of this pamphlet Neale received the only offer of preferment which was destined to come his way—an invitation from the Canons of St Ninian's, Perth, to become the first Dean of their newly-erected Cathedral.[1] The offer was reinforced by a warm letter from the aged Bishop Torry of St Andrew's expressing the hope that he might see fit to accept. It was an aspiration shared by many Scottish Churchmen. 'You have no idea', wrote Neale to a friend, 'of the number of letters I receive from Scotland'.

He had long taken a lively interest in the Scottish Episcopal Church, he had rejoiced in the renewal of vigour in her spiritual life, and he had whole-heartedly given his approval to Bishop Torry's current revision of the Scottish Prayer Book. The consequences of the Gorham judgement still pressing upon him,

[1]In fact only a small part of the cathedral had been built in 1850.

Neale even envisaged a situation in which Catholic-minded Anglicans might be constrained to separate themselves from communion with the See of Canterbury and seek refuge in the ancient Church of St Ninian, St Kentigern and St Columba.

Nevertheless, despite his deep veneration for the Scottish Church and the manifest attractions of the pioneer work which the office would entail, Neale felt himself reluctantly forced to decline the offer of the Perth Deanery. To cross the Border at this moment of crisis in English Church affairs would, it seemed to him, be an act of desertion. Except he and those who thought with him were to abide in the ship she could scarcely be saved from Erastian infidelity. Furthermore, he felt that Scotland's greatest need was for missionary-minded priests who were blessed with the physical stamina to live and work as pioneers.

'I would not come,' he wrote in his letter declining the appointment, 'without a licence from the Bishop to preach anywhere and everywhere—in lanes, streets, markets, fields or roads; that, I am sure, is the only way to convert Scotland. But if I were to do this effectively I should be dead in a year, and that without any adequate advantage gained.'

Finally, he considered that a Dean should be possessed of some acquaintance with the technicalities of music and 'I have a zeal for it, but not according to knowledge'. In spite of his decision not to accept the Deanery, Neale continued to maintain his interest in the Scottish Church and its affairs, and in 1856 he published *The Life and Times of Patrick Torry, D.D., with an Appendix on the Scotch Liturgy.* Bishop Torry had died three years earlier, after an episcopate of forty-four years.

*   *   *

In 1851, in addition to numerous literary undertakings— translations of medieval hymns, books for children, collections of sermons and essays, tracts for the Camden Society, and so forth—Neale accepted an invitation from Beresford-Hope to become a regular contributor to the *Morning Chronicle.* He undertook to write three leaders a week and, since the remuneration was good, this excursion into quasi-secular journalism enabled him to afford a governess for his children.

About this time the tenor of life at Sackville College was rudely disturbed by a sudden further eruption of Protestant fanaticism. The occasion was an excuse rather than a reason. Neale had for a considerable period sought to introduce locally a measure of funeral reform. Contemporary custom demanded that the dead should be laid to rest with the gloomiest and most pagan funereal trappings—black-draped hearses, nodding horse-plumes and top-hatted mutes. Not only were these ostentatious manifestations of grief basically un-Christian in their virtual denial or ignoring of the sure and certain hope of resurrection; they were also excessively costly and their provision bore hardly upon all but the well-to-do.

Deeply concerned at this state of affairs, Neale had written to the *Ecclesiologist* advocating the formation of a burial guild on the lines of the Continental *Misericordia*; he had also tried to establish a more seemly and less expensive usage at Sackville College by providing a bier and a pall. This modest arrangement was seized upon by very influential if not very scrupulous persons in the neighbourhood as yet another example of the dangerous 'Romanizing' activities of the warden. Relatives of deceased inmates of the College who had been buried with these simple and seemly adjuncts instead of the usual pagan pomps were persuaded that their departed dear ones had been deprived of their rights and laid to rest with papal and superstitious observances. Protestant prejudices were then more easily stimulated than they are today, the rustic mind more ignorant and more easily swayed by specious speeches and insinuations. As the poison began to work in slow-thinking and suspicious minds, malice and mischief inevitably sought their opportunity.

It came with the funeral of one of the pensioners. Urged on by trouble-makers who remained discreetly in the background, a crowd of drink-inflamed ruffians broke into the College grounds, seized the coffin from the bearers and bore it with alcoholic triumph to the village inn. As the excitement grew and the ale flowed freely, the habitual rural calm of an English village gave way to an utterly alien and uncharacteristic orgy of bonfire-lighting, window smashing and general hooliganism. Only the timely arrival of the police and the arrest of the ringleaders brought a cessation of these disgraceful proceedings. The malice and bigotry which underlay this squalid outbreak of unreasoning violence greatly saddened Neale. Misrepresentation is always difficult to bear with; when it emanates from those one has laboured to benefit, the sense of frustration becomes even more insupportable.

Furthermore, when mud has been flung and from whatever quarter, a varying proportion of it tends to stick. For the rest of his life Neale was to be the undeserving victim of suspicion and distrust on the part of many who should have been his strongest supporters. He was to know what it is to be wounded in the house of one's friends, and only his firmly-founded faith allied to a naturally friendly and resilient temperament enabled him to rise superior to the hostility he incurred.

It was with relief and exemplary detachment that Neale turned from controversial matters to his unfailing interest in hymnology. As we have already noted, he had possessed from his earliest years a 'fatal facility', to use Webb's expression, for versifying. This had led him to greet with enthusiasm the growing popularity of hymn-singing in English churches. In this he found himself at odds with his old friend Webb, a purist to whom it was a question of the ancient office Hymns in the original tongue or none at all.

The astonishing success of Keble's *The Christian Year*, which in the twenty-six years since its publication had sold 108,000 copies and run into forty-three editions, pointed to a widespread enthusiasm for religious verse. There were, however, at this time few hymns suitable for singing at the services of the Established Church, the only considerable collection bound within one cover being the *Olney Hymnal*, published in 1779 and associated principally with John Newton and William Cowper. These hymns, of a subjective, emotional character for the most part, enjoyed no very wide popularity outside the more Evangelical circles.

In 1827 was published the posthumous *Hymns Written and adapted to the Weekly Church Services of the Year*, the legacy of Reginald Heber, Bishop of Calcutta. To this collection we owe such established favourites as 'Brightest and Best of the Sons of the Morning', 'From Greenland's Icy Mountains', 'Holy, Holy, Holy; Lord God Almighty', 'The Son of God goes forth to War', 'God that madest earth and Heaven', and 'Bread of the World in Mercy Broken'. In 1852 appeared the first part of *The Hymnal Noted*; the second part two years later. This was followed in 1861 by *Hymns Ancient and Modern* which, having set the pattern of Victorian hymn-singing, still retains its popularity in many quarters. To this collection, as of course to its more modern rival *The English Hymnal*, Neale was a prolific contributor, mostly of translations of ancient Greek and Latin office Hymns. Of the 779 hymns in the 1889 edition (with Second Supplement) of *Hymns Ancient and Modern*, no fewer than sixty-four are accredited to Neale; and of 656 in the *English Hymnal*, seventy-two are from his pen.[1] When we are faced with such an output, it is difficult and perhaps invidious to select particular hymns for special mention. Every regular churchgoer will have his or her favourites, and will reject with indignation any list which does not include them all. Nevertheless, a selection must be made if an account of Neale's life and work is to make sense, and for the avoidance of all scruple and occasion of cavil let us enumerate at least one of Neale's translations for each of the Church's seasons and other special occasions, thus:—

Advent: 'Creator of the stars of night'.
Christmas: 'A great and mighty wonder'.
Epiphany: 'How vain the cruel Herod's fear'.
Septuagesima: 'Alleluya, song of sweetness'.
Lent: 'The fast, as taught by holy lore'.
Passiontide: 'The royal banners forward go'.
Palm Sunday: 'All glory, laud and honour'.
Easter: 'Ye Choirs of New Jerusalem'; 'Come, ye faithful, raise the strain'.
Ascension: 'Eternal Monarch, King most high'.
Whitsuntide: 'Come, Thou holy Paraclete'.
Trinity: 'O Trinity of blessed light'.
Dedication Festival: 'Blessed city, Heavenly Salem'.

[1] Out of 105 hymns in the first part of the *Hymnal Noted* published in 1852, 94 were translations by Neale from Latin originals.

Feasts of Apostles: 'The eternal gifts of Christ the King'.

St Mary the Virgin: 'The God Whom earth and sea and sky'.

St Michael and All Angels: 'Stars of the morning, so gloriously bright'.

All Saints: 'If there be that skills to reckon'.

Morning: 'Now that the daylight fills the sky'.

Evening: 'Before the ending of the day'; 'The day is past and over'.

Holy Communion: 'Of the glorious Body telling'; 'The Word of God proceeding forth'.

General: 'Brief life is here our portion'; 'Come, ye faithful, raise the anthem'; 'Jerusalem the golden'; 'Light's abode, celestial Salem'.

Original Compositions: 'O happy band of pilgrims'; 'Art thou weary, art thou languid'.

Such a necessarily restricted list does at least give some idea of the magnificence of Neale's contribution to English hymnology. If his own original contributions were comparatively sparse, it must be acknowledged that in his splendid translations of so many of the ancient hymns of Christendom he tapped a rich and indispensable vein of liturgical poetry, and by so doing laid the English-speaking Christian world eternally in his debt. Only to one who was at once a sound classicist and competent liturgiologist could such an achievement have proved possible. Archbishop Trench of Dublin wrote, in his preface to his 'Sacred Latin Poetry' (1864),

> by patient research in almost all European lands, he (Neale) has brought to light a multitude of hymns unknown before; in a treatise on sequences properly so called, he has for the first time explained their essential character, while to him the English reader owes versions of some of the best hymns, such as often successfully overcome the almost insuperable difficulties which some of them present to the translator.

The volume entitled *Medieval Hymns and Sequences* (1851) represents the fruit of Neale's researches allied to his almost uncanny facility for transliteration. It is said that he would frequently read to the East Grinstead Sisters, *in perfect English,* lessons of which he had before him only the Latin text. This remarkable aptitude led on one occasion to a little innocent leg-pull at the expense of his saintly contemporary, John Keble. The latter had sought Neale's advice over some hymns which he, Keble, had written and proposed to include in a new published collection. Neale journeyed to Hursley Vicarage where he was shown the new compositions. He was then left alone for a short time while Keble went in search of some further papers. When he returned Neale said reproachfully that he had understood Keble's work to be original. So it was, declared the indignant author. 'Then how do you explain this?' demanded Neale, and placed before his host a perfectly turned Latin version of one of the Keble hymns. The distressed and unsuspecting poet could only protest that he had never before seen the Latin 'original'. Then, to his relief and astonishment, Neale admitted that he had translated the lines from English into Latin in the few minutes that Keble had been absent from the room!

*   *   *

The Sussex countryside immediately surrounding East Grinstead was, in the middle of the nineteenth century, sparsely inhabited and poorly provided for, by modern standards at least, in the matter of spiritual ministrations. The district formed part of the Ashdown Forest and as a result of widespread felling of timber had become largely a waste land of heath and scrub. The few farms and cottages were scattered and isolated, far from church or chapel and indeed from even the simplest amenities of civilized living. The inhabitants, who rarely saw a priest or any other visible sign of the Church militant here on earth, existed without opportunity, possibly without conscious desire, for worship or sacramental grace.

Nor were their physical needs any more adequately catered for. In time of sickness neither doctor nor skilled nursing nor medical aids were to be had without a walk of several miles over rough roads or trackways, and not always even then. It was indeed a waste land, spiritually and materially, upon which Neale looked out from his study window in Sackville College.

The farms and cottages were doubtless picturesque and attractive to the outward eye, but inwardly they were insanitary hovels where the simplest hygiene presented intractable problems and the ordinary decencies of life hardly less so. For all their thatched and whitewashed charm, only too often they were breeding grounds of physical disease and moral degradation. Lacking the lavish assistance of the Welfare State, or even the semi-feudal charitable attentions of hall and rectory, their unfortunate inmates remained sunk in the squalor of unameliorated poverty, and no man cared for their souls.

No man, that is, but John Mason Neale, who was haunted by what he knew of their condition and longed to find some means of alleviating it. With his mind steeped in the spirit of medieval religion, it is perhaps not surprising that his thoughts should have turned towards monasticism—to the charity dispensed in the ages of faith at abbey gate, buttery and infirmary; to the evangelization of the remote rural districts of the Chablais by St Francis de Sales; to the care of sick and poor by the Sisters of Charity founded by St Vincent de Paul.

It was as a consequence of his reflections upon this theme that Neale determined upon the founding of an Anglican Sisterhood which would minister to the sick, the lonely and the under-privileged. The revival of the Religious Life for women in the Anglican Communion was a direct result of the Oxford Movement. It had begun in 1841 when Dr Pusey received the vows of Marian Hughes, who became the first Superior of the Convent of the Holy Trinity at Oxford. The first Community was established at Park Village, Regent's Park, in 1845 and was later merged in the Society of the Holy Trinity founded by Miss Sellon at Devonport. There followed in quick succession the Communities of St Thomas the Martyr, Oxford (1847), St Mary the Virgin, Wantage (1848), the Community of All Saints (1851), and the Society of St John the Baptist, Clewer (1852).

Neale sought the advice of Canon T. T. Carter of Clewer, Canon Butler of Wantage and Mother Harriet Monsell of the Clewer Sisterhood, and encouraged by their wise counsel then looked for a hospital which would provide nursing tuition for the Sisterhood he hoped to found. Westminster Hospital offered him what he wanted and lodgings were put at his disposal by the Master of St John's House.

Apart from those pioneers in the Anglican monastic revival already mentioned, Neale had the warm support of a number of prominent Churchmen, lay and clerical; among them Lord Salisbury, W. J. Bennett of Frome and Father Benson of Cowley. The Bishop of Chichester surprisingly extended his blessing upon the project, and Archdeacon Otter helped actively with the drafting of the Rule. Neale himself drew up books of devotions for the use of the Sisters—*A Horology of the Passion, The Hours of the Holy Ghost* and a book of prayers and meditations entitled *The Virgin's Lamp*. Among the first of those who came forward to join the infant Community was the daughter of the aged Rector of Rotherfield. With her were two other women who desired to live lives of consecrated service and who, like her, had a close acquaintance with the material and spiritual conditions of Sussex rural life. From such small beginnings has grown, during the course of a hundred years, a Community which, in addition to its primary purpose of providing opportunities for those who feel called to the Religious Life of fulfilling their vocation, numbers amongst its active works schools, orphanages, hospitals, convalescent homes, parochial mission houses and rescue shelters. Its sound and its daughters have gone out into all lands, and branch houses of the Society of St Margaret are to be found today in such widely scattered parts of Britain and the globe as Cardiff, Brighton, Ventnor, Colombo, Johannesburg, Dundee, Chiswick, Clapham, Chesterfield, Lindfield, Cambridge, Aberdeen, Walsingham and Boston (U.S.A.).

From those early days, when the first Sisters laboured heroically amongst the insanitary hovels of east Sussex and Kent, fighting cholera, smallpox, scarlet fever and diphtheria outbreaks, the Society has continued to fulfil its Founder's most cherished desire that it should regard the relief and, where possible, the cure of disease and suffering as one of its primary obligations. Like St Vincent's Sisters of Charity and the Visitation nuns of St Francis de Sales, the East Grinstead Sisters have been the instruments of the Divine Healer and Sanctifier at countless beds of suffering, sickness or death. Wherever their name and work is known it is inevitably held in highest honour —a remote cry indeed from those early days when a poor sick woman to whom they sought to minister could protest, 'I will not have any ladies that worship images in my house'. The Church of England is deeply in the debt of John Mason Neale on many accounts; most of all, there can be little doubt, for the incomparable legacy he provided in founding the Society of St Margaret.

*   *   *

In 1857 nine orphaned girls were sent to East Grinstead by Neale's sister, Miss Elizabeth Neale, who had gathered them under her care at a Home in Brighton which she was now re-linquishing in order to start a new Sisterhood at St George's-in-the-East, London.[1] The Sisters at St Margaret's Convent gladly welcomed these necessitous children and so was started St Katharine's—an important branch of the Society's work and a source of deep joy and satisfaction to its Founder. Neale loved being with children and it was his delight to celebrate on week-days in the little chapel at the Home, to catechize its inmates, to tell them stories of his own concocting and generally to share their simple joys and sorrows. Sometimes, in summer, he would take them for long rambles in the surrounding Sussex country-side, opening their eyes to some of the wonders to be read in Nature's pages or exploring the 'little lost Down churches' amidst the silent hills. His own children,[2] too, found unfailing delight in his company, his tales and the expeditions he loved to organize. In their deep affection for so loving a parent, they even strove to enter into his somewhat austere and esoteric en-thusiasms. Nine-year-old Agnes faced unflinchingly the task of compiling an *Alphabet of Heresies*; another, when she was 7, was regaled with an account of the Council of Ephesus, and for lighter reading there was their father's translation of the *Moral Concordances* of St Anthony of Padua. One scarcely knows which

[1] This sisterhood later developed into the Community of the Holy Cross.
[2] He had five—a boy and four girls.

to admire the more—the single-minded courage of the parent unafraid to provide so formidable a literary diet, or the fortitude of the children who could take it at such a tender age. There was a spiritual and intellectual toughness about the Victorians which one cannot but admire, however much one may deplore some of the circumstances which called it into play. How many modern ten-year-old children, one wonders, would undertake the mastery of Syriac in order to help a father correct the manuscript of his *Commentary on the Psalms*?

In this work Neale received also the more mature collaboration of Dr Littledale who, for several years, spent Holy Week and Easter at Sackville College. Both were considerable biblical scholars and literary practitioners of no small skill. A deep and sincere spirit of devotion underlay their work which is steeped in spiritual knowledge, patristic profundity and liturgical lore. Subsequent ages have hailed the industry and erudition which the two learned authors brought to this formidable undertaking, but their predominantly mystical treatment of the Psalter does not always commend itself to a more critical contemporary and exegetical approach.[1]

*   *   *

In 1860 the University of Hartford, Connecticut, conferred upon Neale an honorary Doctorate of Divinity. He was modestly gratified by this graceful recognition of his literary achievements—a rare enough experience for one more accustomed to criticism than acclaim. The austere Webb, however, thought he should have declined the honour, fearing that it might expose his friend to the scorn of ill-wishers here in England. Neale explained his acceptance by a refusal to hurt the feelings of those who desired to honour him. His attitude was that of Southey in accepting the Laureateship—it might not be an honour at the time of receiving it, but if God gave him life and health he would make it so.

Although by this time the Sisterhood had become established and generally accepted for its devoted work amongst the

[1]The work, unfinished at Neale's death, was completed by Dr Littledale and published in 4 vols. in 1868.

disease-stricken and the poor, anti-Catholic fanaticism had one
final disgraceful fling. At the burial of a Sister of the Society in
her family's tomb in Lewes, in November 1857, a hostile mob,
drawn from the most criminal and ruffianly elements in the
town, swarmed menacingly into the churchyard. During the
service they shouted and catcalled outside, and when the
cortège appeared they surged violently forward. Neale was
knocked down and trampled on, the Sisters were hustled and
insulted, and only the timely arrival of the police enabled them
to escape, without further harm, to the comparative safety of
the schoolmaster's house. The whole squalid incident had been
engineered by the dead Sister's father. Enraged by the fact that
she had bequeathed her modest fortune partly to the Community and partly to a favourite brother, her father alleged
that she had been trapped into entering the Sisterhood, had
been forced to make a will favouring the Community and had
been deliberately exposed to infection in her nursing duties.
Unbelievably, the Bishop of Chichester lent a credulous ear to
these calumnies and withdrew from his position as Visitor to
the Community, in spite of remonstrances from influential
friends and supporters of Neale such as Lord Richard Caven-
dish. His true friends stood by him as at all times but, once
more, some of the flung mud adhered and for the time being the
Community suffered a considerable loss of support.

This was quickly made good, however, and fresh opportunities of work for the Sisters were continually forthcoming. There
was a House of Refuge to be opened at Ash near Aldershot, a
daughter Sisterhood to be launched in Aberdeen, a smallpox
hospital to be staffed at Salisbury. Each new commitment
meant an increasing burden of responsibility upon the already
over-weighted shoulders of a man who never had enjoyed
robustness of health.

In addition he was in constant demand as preacher, lecturer,
confessor, and conductor of retreats from all over the country.
Seldom did he refuse a request that it was humanly possible for
him to accede to, and inevitably nature exacted her penalty.
In the early part of 1886 unmistakable signs of physical ex-
haustion manifested themselves, chills and indispositions be-

came more frequent. Yet Neale permitted himself no abate-
ment of his labours. In all weathers, in journeyings oft, he
struggled to fulfil an ever-increasing list of engagements while
deeply immersed in the administration of Sackville College, the
Community and its ramifications.

At last the flesh rebelled against the burden. Throughout
the spring and summer of 1866 Neale was forced to accept the
fact that he had overdrawn on his balance of physical resources.
On Refreshment Sunday, 11 March, Mrs Neale received a
touching letter from John Keble sympathizing with her over her
husband's incapacity. Less than three weeks later, on Maundy
Thursday, Keble himself died, and although he was able to
write in eulogy of the revered Tractarian leader, Neale was
soon to follow him through the valley of the shadow. As the
waving corn turned to gold beneath the Sussex Downs, he
passed beyond all praise and blame, on the Feast of the Trans-
figuration, 6 August.

These words from one of the best-known and best-loved of all
his hymns may serve as epitaph and valediction.

> If I find Him, if I follow,
> What His guerdon here?
> Many a sorrow, many a labour,
>   Many a tear.
>
> If I still hold closely to Him,
> What hath He at last?
> Sorrow vanquished, labour ended,
>   Jordan past.
>
> Finding, following, keeping, struggling,
> Is He sure to bless?
> Angels, Martyrs, Prophets, Virgins,
>   Answer 'Yes.'

CHAPTER VII

POST-TRACTARIAN PROPHET

THE century and a quarter which have elapsed since the beginning of the Oxford Movement with Keble's sermon on National Apostasy in 1833 have witnessed the most profound changes in the life of our nation—social, political and economic. So, too, for the Church of England it has proved a period of transformation and evolution, with fresh problems constantly arising, and new dangers sometimes threatening, but also with new opportunities opening up on every side.

The main problems with which the Church has had to contend during this period are very largely concerned with Money and Manpower, but other issues of a more intellectual or spiritual kind have given rise to periodical crises. The effect of two world wars upon the purchasing power of the pound sterling has had a serious effect upon the efficiency of a Church so largely dependent upon endowments. The principal victims of this apparently interminable process are, of course, the parochial clergy, the majority of whom wrestle daily with the problem of trying to meet present-day costs of living out of stipends barely adequate for the purpose in pre-war days.

Then there is the decline, partially halted in the past few years, in the number of young men offering themselves for the Church's ministry. This decline is only partly due to the difficulty of making ends meet and to the unmanageable nature of the houses and grounds which the clergy are required to occupy and maintain. We must look deeper for the chief reason—to the general spiritual decline apparent throughout the country during the past hundred years. It is not only the Church of England, of course, which has felt the effect of this decline, but since it was the Church which most people formerly attended and to which indeed a majority of English Christians still profess some degree of nominal attachment, it now enjoys the dubious distinction of being the Church from which most English folk stay away.

Yet the picture, sombre though it may appear, is not one of unrelieved depression and gloom. There is much to be thankful for as well as much to deplore. The silver linings are there all right behind the clouds. To conclude that the Church of England is dead and done for, or that she is slowly dying on her feet, would be vastly wide of the mark. She is an anvil which has worn out many hammers, and she has a disconcerting habit of confounding the predictions of her impending dissolution by quite suddenly exhibiting signs of renewed life and vitality astonishing in one so allegedly near her appointed end.

In the post-war years we have seen a distinct evidence of such rejuvenation in the improvement in the numbers of those being baptized, confirmed and ordained, as also in her general financial position. These, perhaps, are secondary matters and only imperfect indications of the Church's spiritual state. But indications of a definite kind they are, and their significance should not be overlooked. There is a considerable amount still of loose talk about 'empty churches' (where are they, one wonders?) but little is heard about the well-attended ones up and down the country. There may be fewer people in our churches than there were a century ago, but, it must be reiterated, there are almost certainly more—considerably more—in them who are there because they want to be; who are there from conviction and not from convention. If the quantity of churchgoers has declined over the century, the quality has undoubtedly increased.

So, too, has the quality of the services themselves—whatever may be said of the sermons. The conduct of divine worship generally is more seemly and dignified, the sacraments are more highly valued and more suitably administered; the musical standard is higher and so is that of the artistic settings and accessories of public worship. These, again, may be matters of lesser moment, but they are important signs of an ever-growing

sense amongst Anglicans that to worship the Lord in the beauty
of holiness is to perform an act of paramount significance, an
act which calls for the best that man can give of time, money,
materials and skill in the service of the sanctuary.

In spite of all the setbacks and difficulties with which she has
had to contend, the Anglican Church can look back, not indeed
with any kind of complacency, but at least with the firm conviction that under God she has been able to record some
notable progress on several fronts and so has been enabled to
make her contribution to the advancement of the Kingdom.
She can indeed look back with gratitude over a hundred years
of divinely guided endeavour in the mission field at home and
abroad, in the sphere of religious education, in revived parochial activity, in the development of her corporate sense of
social responsibility, in the successful revival of the Religious
Life in its technical sense, and in the extension of such highly
valuable religious activities as retreats, quiet days, parochial
and liturgical missions, pilgrimages and study groups. Considerable opportunities have presented themselves and have
been widely used of applying modern means of communication
and instruction to the task of propagating the Faith. Religious
works continue to form the largest category of new books published each year, the ubiquitous parish magazine goes into
hundreds of thousands of homes, religious drama reaches a
higher standard of production each year and plays a notable
part in spreading religious truth through a medium which has
been popular since the Middle Ages, religious broadcasting has
long been established, religious films and film strips make slow
if unspectacular progress, and 'tele-religion' has now reared its
sometimes controversial head.

But perhaps the most important achievement of the Church
over the past hundred years or so has been its ever-increasing
concern with the great problems—private and public—of
everyday life. Faced with the pressing questions of the day—
questions concerning work, leisure, money, marriage, home
life, housing, health, education, international affairs—the
Church and her leaders have attempted, not always successfully or acceptably it must be admitted, to apply to them the

spiritual and moral principles explicitly or implicitly consequent upon their Faith. It has been their endeavour to make
clear that the Church's Gospel is universal in its application
and of practical validity in every department of life; that it is
not a pleasant, part-time occupation for the ecclesiastically-
minded, but a practical necessity for every man who is conscious of being more than animal; a guiding light which the
nations of the world can only disregard to the ultimate peril of
all humanity.

During the period under review the Church of England has
thrown up many men of outstanding ability and leadership,
men possessing supreme spiritual and intellectual qualities who
have made tremendous contributions to the work of the Church
in its widely-varied manifestations. A volume at least would be
required to render due praise to all these famous men. Here
they must be represented by one to whom perhaps more than to
any other the Church of England in the twentieth century owes
an immeasurable debt; one who not only dominated the religious thinking of his day but whose influence survives, whether
acknowledged or not, into our own time and, if one might
prophesy, will continue to do so far into the unforeseeable
future.

*   *   *

Charles Gore was born at Wimbledon on 2 January 1853,
the fourth son of a senior member of the Civil Service. On his
father's side he was a great-grandson of the second Earl of
Arran, while his maternal grandfather was the fourth Earl of
Bessborough. It will be seen from this that his social antecedents
were aristocratic; his religious ones, on his own testimony, were
the conventional Low Church outlook of his day and milieu.
Religion attracted him from an early age, and in later years
his sister recalled him, at the age of 8 or thereabouts, clad in
a nightgown, preaching a sermon from behind a towel horse to
the other occupants of the nursery.

After three years at a preparatory school near Malvern,
Charles went to Harrow in 1866, joining there his next elder
brother Spencer—a brilliant games player who was later to

become the first All England Lawn Tennis champion. Charles himself was only an average athlete, but he quickly gave evidence of his mental ability, rapidly reaching a remarkably high standard of classical scholarship. At Harrow, Gore came under the influence of B. F. Westcott, then an assistant master at the school, later Bishop of Durham and a biblical scholar of international repute. He also formed close and lasting friendships with several boys who shared with him his dissatisfaction at the prevailing Low Church religious atmosphere of the school. There was then no weekly celebration of the Holy Communion in the school chapel, and Gore and his friends formed the habit of attending the Eucharist on Sunday mornings at the parish church.

During holidays from Harrow, Gore found his way to various famous centres of 'ritualism'—St Michael's, Shoreditch, for example, and St Alban's, Holborn, where he saw the Mass performed with full splendour—vestments, incense, banners, and the *Hallelujah Chorus* thrown in at the end, after a 'magnificent sermon' by the great and greatly-loved Father Stanton. It was this devoted priest who taught young Gore 'to make his confession, to love the Mass and to fast on Fridays'. From thenceforth there was for him but one Faith and one way of worship, and to the end of his long life he remained firmly and passionately attached to the Catholic Faith as taught and practised within the Church of England.

From Harrow he went with a scholarship to Balliol, where the great Jowett was Master, taking with him a considerable classical repute. In his last school term he had carried off prizes for Greek epigram, Latin essay and elegiacs, as well as for modern history and English literature. Among his contemporaries at Balliol who were afterwards to achieve highest honours in their chosen avocations were Alfred Milner, H. H. Asquith, Herbert Warren, and T. A. Lacey.

At Oxford, Gore's social and political conscience was awakened, and he spoke frequently and fiercely in Union Debates on such matters as trades unionism and in support of Mr Gladstone's Liberal Government, often finding himself in a Radical minority with Asquith. He also attended services at the

Church of the Cowley Fathers in the Iffley Road, and formed a deep admiration for Father R. M. Benson and the great Community (Society of St John the Evangelist) which he had founded. Thus was Gore brought to appreciate the tremendous value to the English Church of what is technically known as the 'Religious Life' under the threefold vows of poverty, obedience and chastity—a circumstance which was to have important consequences at a later stage of his career. His closest friends, who shared his religious and political views, were G. W. E. Russell, with whom he had been at Harrow, and Henry Scott Holland, a near neighbour at Wimbledon and afterwards Canon of St Paul's Cathedral. Later Edward Talbot was admitted to the inner circle of Gore's friends, but it is doubtful whether anyone ever held the place in his affections which Scott Holland occupied until his death in 1918.

Gore took First Classes in Classical Moderations and in Greats, and in 1875 he was elected Fellow of Trinity. As a don he seems to have been delightfully original and unacademic. His remarkably youthful appearance frequently led to his being mistaken for a freshman and once to his being invited by the Captain of Boats to come down to the river for his rowing potentialities to be overlooked. There was nothing immature in his thought or conversation, however, and the forthrightness of his view was invariably reflected in his speech. He was always most temperate in his habits, but decidedly no Puritan. Once, when offered tea by a rabidly teetotal bishop's wife, he is reputed to have replied, 'Thank you, but I never drink anything but alcoholic beverages'. Politically, while always striving to be fair and unprejudiced in his judgements, he could not conceal his deep distrust of Mr Disraeli—whom he regarded as 'clever but unscrupulous'—nor his profound admiration of Mr Gladstone.

Gore was ordained deacon in Advent, 1876, and priest two years later. During this period of his life he formed one of a group of friends who for a month every summer took charge of some small country parish, making themselves responsible for all parochial duty, reciting the daily offices and occupying their days with reading and discussion. This group, of which Scott

Holland, J. R. Illingworth and Francis Paget (later Bishop of Oxford) were also members, was humorously known as 'The Holy Party' and it was during one of their annual discussions that the project was first mooted of forming an Anglican Religious Order for priests on the lines of the Oratorians.

After his ordination as priest Gore felt the need to exercise more fully the pastoral side of his ministry and for a time he worked during the vacations as unlicensed curate of the parish of Christ Church, Bootle, at the same time of course retaining his Fellowship and his teaching activities at Oxford during term. A little later he worked in the parish of St. Margaret's, Princes Road, Liverpool, where he found himself greatly absorbed in the various social activities that flourished, and particularly in a club for men on whose behalf he was mainly instrumental in obtaining permanent premises. It was the incumbent of this same parish, the Reverend H. Bell Cox, who was later prosecuted under the infamous Public Worship Regulation Act and sent to prison for wearing Eucharistic vestments.

At some time during this period of his life Gore grew the beard which he wore for the remainder of his days. He found it, he says, hard to cultivate in its early stages, and only succeeded eventually by 'meditating a great deal on the Four Last Things'!

★　　　★　　　★

In 1880, only four years after his ordination, Gore was offered, by Bishop Mackarness of Oxford, the post of Vice-Principal of Cuddesdon Theological College. Here was scope for him to exercise his undoubted powers of influencing young men while, at the same time, participating in teaching work of a definitely pastoral and theological kind. He gladly accepted the offer and took up his new position in July, 1880. The three years which followed were tremendously happy ones for Gore and vitally important ones for the College. Since the great days of its saintly founder, Dr King, later Bishop of Lincoln, Cuddesdon had experienced a period of comparative leanness. With Gore's coming, however, a new spirit was infused into the place. His brilliant scholarship, inspired teaching, genius for friendship and ever-present sense of fun captivated the students, and gradually restored the College to its former position of pre-eminence amongst Anglican theological colleges. Side by side with all his hard work in the College, Gore became increasingly in demand as a preacher and lecturer in numerous places beyond its walls. So well-known did he become in this respect that his activities gave rise to the witticism that 'Cuddesdon is more celebrated for its Vices than for its Principals'!

In September 1882, the great Dr Pusey died. Although for many years past he had lived the life of a virtual recluse in his rooms in Christ Church, he had always been revered, next to Keble, as the foremost of the founders of the Oxford Movement, certainly as the Revival's greatest scholar. He was venerated alike for his personal sanctity, his massive learning, his fearless leadership in the days when the Movement was under constant attack from every side, and for the persecution he had endured on behalf of the Church's Faith. After his death a memorial fund was inaugurated under the sponsorship of some of Pusey's leading friends and admirers, foremost among whom were Charles Wood (later Lord Halifax), Lord Beauchamp, Sir Walter Phillimore and H. P. Liddon, Canon of St Paul's and Pusey's most devoted disciple. Within a year of the launching of the fund a sum of £25,000 was contributed and substantially more money came in later. It was decided, mainly at Liddon's instigation, to use the money for the establishment in Oxford of an institution for theological research, staffed by priests who would act as teachers of theology free from university or collegiate restrictions and also as pastoral advisers and friends to Anglican undergraduates. The result was the opening, in 1883, of Pusey House with Gore as its first Principal and V. S. Stuckey Coles and F. E. Brightman to assist him. Since the Governors of Pusey House had used part of the Memorial Fund to purchase Dr Pusey's vast theological library to be housed in the building which bore his name and was to perpetuate his memory, these assistants were to be known as Librarians.

Gore and his two chosen henchmen, while revered for their outstanding qualities, were suspect on the part of the more theologically conservative members of the university as being dangerously 'liberal' and 'advanced' in some of their biblical and social theories. Dr Pusey himself had been strongly opposed to what was known as the Higher Criticism and Gore's appointment was regarded by this section of opinion as, to say the least, a doubtful way of paying tribute to the memory of the great Tractarian. Someone expressed this uneasiness in a satirical little parody.

> Sing a song of thousands,
> Thirty, say, or more,
> Spent in subsidizing
> Brightman, Stuckey, Gore.
> When the House was opened
> Stewart Headlam came—
> Wasn't that a pretty thing
> To do in Pusey's name?

Nevertheless Gore stayed for ten years in what in his lighter moments he referred to as the 'Puseum', and this decade proved to be a most fruitful one, pastorally and scholastically. In the course of it he wrote *The Church and the Ministry*, in which he examined and expounded the origins of the Christian Ministry and its development in the sub-apostolic age. This scholarly work was well received by contemporary ecclesiastical historians, such as Lightfoot and Wordsworth, and subsequently went into several editions. So also did a shorter book entitled *Roman Catholic Claims* in which Gore sought to refute the anti-Anglican arguments of one, Luke Rivington, who had recently seceded to the Church of Rome.

In 1887 Gore founded the Society of the Resurrection, a priestly fellowship with a rule of life which included regular prayer, simplicity of life and an undertaking, renewable annually, to remain single. Its principal purposes were to deepen the spiritual life of priests at home and to encourage clerical interest in the work of the Oxford Mission to Calcutta, something of whose heroic labours Gore had seen on a visit to India in 1884. Gore became the Society's first Superior, and it provided him with a further opportunity for that pastoral work in which he always found the deepest spiritual satisfaction.

Two years later the Christian Social Union came into being,

with Gore's former schoolmaster Westcott as its President and
with Gore himself and Scott Holland as Vice-Presidents. This
Society, which rapidly reached a membership of nearly three
thousand, with affiliated branches in the Dominions and United
States, provided Gore with a platform for proclaiming those
ideals of social justice and reform which ever aroused his
keenest enthusiasm. Its principles were soundly based upon the
teaching of the Sermon on the Mount and were disseminated
widely by means of public meetings, lectures and printed propaganda. In all this Gore took a leading part and by so doing
incurred the disapprobation of many, such as Liddon, who
regarded the Union with suspicion on account of what they
conceived to be its subversive tendencies.

Such disapproval, however, was as nothing to the storm of
criticism and condemnation which burst upon Gore in the same
year (1889) when the volume of essays with the title of *Lux
Mundi* appeared under his editorship. These essays were for the
most part an attempt by a group of younger theologians to state
the age-old Faith of Christendom in terms which would commend themselves to contemporary modes of thought and in the
light of the most recent biblical studies and scientific discoveries.
The book's impact was immediate, and unexpectedly sensa-
tional. Liddon denounced the work as 'a proclamation of revolt
against the principles of Dr Pusey and Mr Keble'. Father
Benson of Cowley called it *Lux Mundana* and scandalized old
ladies were led to speak of 'that awful Mr Gore who doesn't
believe the Bible'.

Actually Gore himself, besides editing the volume, had contributed only one essay—on the 'Inspiration of Holy Scripture'
—in which he sought to trace the principle of the development
of knowledge and illumination progressively through the books
of the Old Testament down to the time of our Lord. He emphasized the difference, well known to the early Christian
Fathers, between inspiration and a mechanical or miraculous
communication to the biblical authors of facts which would in
the normal way be beyond their apprehension. In Genesis and
some other parts of the Old Testament the divine inspiration
was to be found, not in the accuracy of the facts and incidents

B.B.—M

related—for these were frequently nothing but primitive folk-lore and legend with no scientific or historical validity—but in the spiritual application of these frequently naïve and anthropomorphic stories in accordance with the needs and knowledge of more intellectually advanced and sophisticated times. The New Testament, as being mainly the work of eye-witnesses or based upon the first-hand information of such, was to be treated rather differently from the Old, but still with an open mind and a willingness 'to follow wheresoever the argument led'. 'It is of the essence of the New Testament, as the religion of the Incarnation, to be final and catholic: on the other hand, it is of the essence of the Old Testament to be imperfect, because it represents a gradual process of education by which man was lifted out of the depths of sin and ignorance.'

What most outraged Gore's critics, however, was the view put forward at the end of his essay that when our Lord took upon Himself our human nature He accepted at the same time certain limitations of earthly knowledge. In the words of St Paul, 'He emptied Himself'. By this 'Kenotic Theory', so called from the Greek word which means 'self-emptying', Gore explained that in his references to the Flood and to Jonah, as well as in attributing to King David certain psalms now widely held to be of much later authorship, our Lord was simply accepting the commonly-held suppositions of His day without prejudice to any subsequent advances in scientific literary or historical knowledge. All this is fairly generally accepted today in all but the most fundamentalist of biblical backwaters, but in 1889 it was revolutionary and profoundly alarming to many.

Gore was greatly disturbed at the distress which he had inadvertently caused to many for whom he had the utmost regard, and although he could not conscientiously withdraw anything he had written—which represented his sincere opinions honestly arrived at after prolonged study and deliberation—he did write to the Governors of Pusey House offering to resign his office as Principal. Bishop Stubbs of Oxford, however, in order that the scandal of a public dispute might be avoided, persuaded Gore to consider his offer of resignation as 'not having been made', and he consequently felt able to continue as Principal. Meanwhile *Lux Mundi* continued to be argued about—and read, both at home and overseas where cheap popular editions were soon called for and issued by John Murray, the publisher.

By 1891 the storm had subsided sufficiently for Gore to be asked to undertake the Bampton Lectures for that year. He gratefully accepted this opportunity of further clarifying publicly his religious thought and in demonstrating his fundamental orthodoxy of belief. The lectures, delivered in Lent, 1891, attracted audiences which filled St Mary's, the University Church, from floor to galleries. Dons and undergraduates packed the pews, stood in the aisles and chapels, or sat on the steps of pulpit and chancel. They listened to a man rich in eloquence, profound in religious thought and knowledge, and imbued with a passionate devotion to the Person Who was the subject of his lectures—which were entitled 'The Incarnation of the Son of God'. These lectures, published in book form later in the year, further enhanced Gore's already considerable reputation and firmly established him among the foremost English theologians of the day. Suspect some of his teachings might be to the ultra-conservative; to the younger generation of theological scholars and students his utterances increasingly acquired a prophetic quality far transcending those of most other contemporary religious teachers.

*   *   *

As the dust of controversy occasioned by the publication of *Lux Mundi* began to settle, Gore was able to turn his attention to another project very near to his heart. This was the inauguration of the new religious community which had been in his mind ever since the founding of the Society of the Resurrection. On 28 July 1892, the first six postulants made their profession of vows and the Community of the Resurrection came into being. In addition to Gore himself, who was elected Superior but preferred to call himself simply 'Senior', the infant Order consisted of James Nash, John Carter, Cyril Bickersteth, George Longridge and Walter Frere. Of these Nash and Frere, and of course Gore himself, subsequently became bishops.

The Community's Rule was framed in such a way as to adapt the traditional monastic principles of chastity, poverty and obedience to modern needs and into an Anglican setting. Its members on entering the Community were to hand over to the common fund all personal possessions and income, but retaining any private capital they might own. Celibacy was to be their intention, but their vows of membership were to be renewed annually. Obedience was to be paid to the Superior within the framework of the Rule. Their dress was to be the ordinary cassock worn by any Anglican priest, nor did they at first use the title of 'Father'. This usage was adopted by the Community at a later date.

The Community began its existence beneath the hospitable roof of Pusey House, but as its numbers grew it quickly became clear that this arrangement could not long continue. It was eventually decided that Gore should resign the Principalship, and that a country parish should be sought where the members of the Community could live together and establish their corporate life free from the distractions inevitable in so frequented a place as Pusey. In the summer of 1893 Gore was offered and accepted the benefice of Radley, a few miles out of Oxford, and thither the Community migrated later in the year. Gore laboured as conscientiously and unremittingly in his rural parish as he had in Oxford or in Liverpool, but the coveted peace and opportunities for serious study were even less forthcoming than they had been at Pusey House. He soon felt that he had made a mistake in accepting a country parish, and at the end of May in 1894 he broke down through the accumulated stress of overwork. He was ordered to take six months' leave of absence from the parish and went to Germany to recuperate. On his return Lord Rosebery, then Prime Minister, offered him the vacant Deanery of Winchester but, feeling that he lacked the necessary administrative and organizing ability for such a post, he refused it. Within a week or so the Prime Minister had offered him a vacant canonry at Westminster, a post he felt was ideally suited to the work he wanted to do. He accepted with profound relief.

The Community, while recognizing that the pulpit of

Westminster Abbey would undoubtedly offer admirable scope for their Superior's prophetic powers, were not convinced that either London or the Abbey were satisfactory surroundings for the nurturing of the religious life. It continued to make its headquarters at Radley until it moved to Mirfield in Yorkshire, in 1898.

As Canon of Westminster, Gore was at the height of his powers, intellectual and oratorical. Sunday after Sunday he attracted great crowds to the Abbey, less by the novelty of his subject than by the forceful sincerity of his utterances. Even Nonconformists, who might have disagreed with the content of his theology, came to hear him and to be fascinated and impressed by the manner of its imparting. Long before the time of service queues began to form outside the Abbey when Gore was preaching, and his hearers filled the great building, the choir and transepts as well as the nave being occupied to overflowing so that within a few minutes of the doors being opened not even standing room was to be found.

His weekday lecture courses, too, were always well attended and many of these resulted in books which enabled his teachings to reach an ever-growing public. In 1896 he published his exposition of *The Sermon on the Mount* and this was followed, at intervals of twelve months or so, by his commentaries on *The Epistle to the Ephesians* and *The Epistle to the Romans*. In 1901 appeared *The Body of Christ*, an exposition of the Sacrament of the Eucharist which came in for a good deal of attack from both Protestant and extreme Anglo-Catholic quarters. The former disapproved of its insistence upon the reality of our Lord's presence in the Sacrament and in the sacrificial nature of its offering; the latter were annoyed by the book's unqualified condemnation of such modern Roman developments in Eucharistic practice as Exposition, Benediction and Processions of the Host.

Gore, from the Abbey pulpit, criticized the imperialistic attitude of the British Government, Press and Public over the dispute with the Boer Republics, but when war broke out in 1899 he occupied himself over the spiritual welfare of the troops, trying hard to secure the appointment of A. F. Winnington-

Ingram, then Bishop of Stepney, as Chaplain-General to the Forces. Lord Roberts promised to use his influence to this end, but before anything could come of the plan Lord Salisbury had appointed Ingram to succeed Mandell Creighton as Bishop of London. Gore also bitterly attacked the establishment of concentration camps in South Africa which had resulted in a high rate of mortality among the Boer women and children who had been herded into them. He sent a strong letter of protest to *The Times*, which the following day printed a violent reply from one of the Canons of Worcester. Within a fortnight it was announced that Gore had been appointed to the vacant Worcester Bishopric.

There was a certain further piquancy in Gore's nomination to a diocese of which the principal centre of population was Birmingham, for this was the political stronghold of Joseph Chamberlain, the Colonial Secretary whose South African policy Gore had so vehemently denounced. As a writer in *The Review of Reviews* put it, it was as though John the Baptist had been appointed by Pontius Pilate to be bishop of Galilee when Herod was at the height of his glory!

Before accepting nomination Gore had of course consulted the other members of the Community. They in turn felt the decision must be his, and after Talbot had urged the arguments in favour of his accepting Gore felt that his course of action was clear. He resigned his office as Superior of the Community, and withdrew from the English Church Union of which he had been a member for nearly thirty years. A diocesan bishop, he felt, should have no attachments of a party or controversial nature. This did not prevent the Church Association (an extreme Protestant organization) from objecting to the confirmation of his election, the egregious Mr Kensit and some of his minions causing a certain amount of tiresome but unproductive disturbance. Gore was consecrated by Archbishop Frederick Temple in the chapel of Lambeth Palace on Sunday, 23 February 1902, and the following afternoon he was enthroned in Worcester Cathedral.

Gore brought to his episcopate all the manifold gifts of heart and mind which had so greatly distinguished him in

Oxford and London. What he did not bring was any considerable love or ability for the administrative side of a bishop's work. Although he tackled it with all his customary conscientiousness, he felt that it constituted a grievous hindrance to the performance of his proper episcopal and pastoral functions. He was resentful of and never fully reconciled to the inroads upon his time and strength made by the day to day routine of diocesan business.

The old Worcester diocese comprised the counties of Worcestershire and Warwickshire, and included the vast urban mass of Birmingham. It was clear to him from the beginning of his episcopate that there would have to be a division of the diocese if the entirely dissimilar needs of its rural and urban components were to be adequately met. In any case, Birmingham was not traditionally a part of the diocese of Worcester and in fact had only been transferred to it from Lichfield in 1836.

An attempt had been made a few years previously to form a separate diocese of Birmingham but little had come of the plan. On Gore's arrival at Worcester, however, the project was revived and received his warmest support. In April 1902 an offer of £10,000 towards the new see was made in a letter sent to *The Times*, and Gore at once undertook to relinquish £800 of his Worcester income towards the endowment and also promised a further £10,000—the whole of the fortune left to him in his mother's will. With such generosity to encourage them, the Church-folk of Birmingham responded with enthusiasm and within a very short time the money needed for the endowment of the new bishopric had been raised. Chamberlain himself, who had come to know and respect Gore, undertook to sponsor the necessary Parliamentary legislation, solely on the understanding that Gore should become Birmingham's first bishop. In spite of some further Protestant opposition, the Bill constituting the new diocese was passed by Parliament and later in the same year Gore's appointment as first Bishop of Birmingham was announced.

Ever a man of the town rather than of the country, Gore found in this great Midland city an atmosphere most congenial to him. He also found his new diocese far more manageable in

size from an administrative point of view. His six years' episcopate was marked by considerable improvements in organization
and a great advance in Church activity. As a consequence of his
leadership, new parochial districts were formed, churches, halls
and vicarages erected, and reinforcements of priests attracted
to the city to cope with the ever-expanding opportunities. With
his warm-hearted sympathy and capacity for making friends,
Gore won the affection of people of every social class and of
widely different interests. Nor were his friendships confined to
Anglican Churchmen. While he never concealed his own very
definite doctrinal and ecclesiastical views, his unfailing courtesy
and consideration towards those who differed from him won
him the respect and affection of Nonconformists of every
variety. He had gone to Birmingham preceded by his reputation as an unyielding High Churchman. The Low Church
clergy of the city found in him a father and a friend who respected their principles, instead of the prelatical autocrat whose
advent they had feared. As a consequence none held him in
deeper regard than they.

In spite of the fact that diocesan organization was a more
practicable proposition in his new diocese, Gore found it no
more to his liking, and steadfastly refused to believe that he was
any good at it. When William Temple, son of the old Archbishop, remarked that everyone told him how well things were
going in Birmingham, Gore triumphantly retorted, 'That only
shows what shocking bad company you keep!'

In the summer of 1911, Gore's old friend Francis Paget,
Bishop of Oxford, died, and Gore was at once offered the vacant
see. He was in great doubt whether to accept or refuse. He was
happy in Birmingham and the thought of the great sprawling
diocese of Oxford, covering three counties and with nearly 700
mainly rural parishes, rather appalled him. On the other hand
and by way of attraction, there was the university, the schools
(Eton, Radley, Bradfield, St Edward's, etc.) the religious houses
(Cowley, Clewer, Wantage) and the fact that his dearest friend,
Henry Scott Holland, was now Regius Professor of Divinity and
ipso facto head of the Oxford faculty of theology. These, he
admitted, were not the highest of motives for accepting and

indeed might well be a reason for declining. Furthermore, in view of the fact that he usually supported the Government in the House of Lords, he was chary of accepting an appointment which might suggest, to the uncharitably-minded, a reward 'for services rendered'. His hesitations were only finally overcome when the Archbishop, Holland and Talbot (now Bishop of Winchester) all urged him to accept translation.

His departure from Birmingham called forth sincere expressions of loyalty and esteem on the part of his clergy, and of heartfelt regret on the part of the lay folk of the diocese, the civic authorities and the Nonconformists with whom he had co-operated so amicably in numerous social and moral causes. The city fathers decided that the episcopate of their first bishop should be commemorated by the erection of a statue of him near the west door of the cathedral. When Gore was informed of their intention he is reputed to have said, 'Please convey to the committee my mingled feelings of gratitude and repugnance'. The praise of men, however deserved and however sincerely proffered, was always deeply distasteful to him.

*   *   *

Gore's Oxford episcopate has sometimes been referred to as a failure, and it is true that he was probably less effective in his unwieldy new rural diocese than he had been in the more compact and mentally stimulating diocese of Birmingham. But success and failure are purely relative terms when applied to such imponderables, and while he may have achieved a less spectacular success as Bishop of Oxford, here, as elsewhere, he laboured abundantly with far-reaching if not immediately obvious consequences.

The rambling and vastly uncomfortable Bishop's 'Palace' at Cuddesdon was just across the road from the Theological College, and it was a great joy to him to renew his connexion with that place, to lecture from time to time to the students, to entertain them to meals at his own table. He visited assiduously the parishes of his huge diocese, invariably preaching in two, often in three of them, most Sundays in the year. His sermons were those of a great scholar, rich with the spoils of a lifetime of wide reading and profundity of thought. Yet they were at the same time the utterances of one who at all times strove to walk humbly with his God and as such were listened to with attentive appreciation by the country folk who came to hear him in the village churches of the Chilterns, the Thames Valley and the Berkshire Downs.

The daily routine began with the Holy Eucharist in his private chapel, celebrated on alternate days by his chaplain and himself. When he was at home they likewise ended in chapel with Compline, after which he would shut himself in his study for an hour or two of uninterrupted reading. He was punctual and methodical in answering correspondence and in dealing with diocesan business, though this was to him, as always, the most irksome side of a bishop's work. Confronted with his morning mail, he was occasionally known to refer wryly to a bishop's lot as 'a dog's life'. He was meticulous in the arrangement and conduct of episcopal functions such as confirmations, consecration of churches and ordinations, and although he was no ceremonialist he insisted that all should be done 'decently and in order'. He found little time for recreation but liked to take brisk walks, when opportunity offered, in the country lanes around Cuddesdon. Sometimes, when returning by car from an episcopal engagement in some distant part of his diocese, he would ask to be put down two or three miles from home so that he could finish the journey on foot.

As Bishop of Oxford Gore continued to take a leading part in movements for social and educational advancement, and once every year he gave an address to the Reading branch of the Workers' Educational Association. This annual engagement afforded him a pleasure as great as his lecture gave to the intelligent artisans who formed his audience. When a dispute arose in 1911 between the management and workers of a large industrial concern in Reading, Gore's sympathies were aroused on behalf of the employees, who he felt were being unfairly treated. He not only sent a contribution to their funds, but was also instrumental in causing an investigation to be made by experts into working conditions in the town generally. The results of this inquiry, when published, showed that over three thousand

Reading families were in receipt of wages insufficient to maintain an adequate standard of living. By his interest and his efforts on their behalf Gore won the gratitude and affection of the workers of the district, most of whom probably had no direct connexion of any kind with organized religion.

Gore's Oxford episcopate was not untroubled by religious controversy. One such dispute came to a head in 1912 and concerned the Anglican Benedictine Community which had established itself a dozen or so years before on Caldey Island off the coast of south Wales. Gore had been invited by the Community (at the insistence of the Archbishop of Canterbury and as a condition of their being officially recognized) to act as Visitor. He reluctantly consented to undertake the duty on condition that their property was legally secured to the Church of England, that the Prayer Book Order of the Mass was followed, that Prayer Book Mattins and Evensong were said daily in addition to any other monastic offices which might be recited and that the Roman services of Exposition and Benediction were discontinued. The Archbishop approved of these requirements and regarded them as eminently reasonable. The Community were persuaded otherwise and all but four, only one of whom was in solemn vows, made their submission to Rome. Gore came in for bitter criticism from some of the more extreme Anglo-Catholics for his handling of the situation and for what Lord Halifax somewhat inappositely termed his 'ultramontane inflexibility'. It was an unfortunate but probably inevitable end to an arrangement which Gore had little confidence would prove to be workable. His strongly-held Anglican convictions would never have permitted him to connive at what he regarded as a thoroughly unsatisfactory situation, ecclesiastically antinomian and liturgically indefensible.

For his own diocese he issued stringent regulations concerning Reservation of the Holy Sacrament. Reservation was to be in both kinds, in a locked chapel inaccessible to the public, and no 'extra-liturgical' services of devotion to the Elements so reserved was permitted. In framing these regulations he was guided less by his own personal inclinations than by what he felt to be expedient. At that time there was still widespread opposition to the practice of Reservation, especially on the part of many of the bishops. Gore felt that the best way to overcome this antagonism was to permit reservation only in such a manner that the more serious of the objections against the practice could not be brought to bear.

Gore was greatly distressed about this time by various manifestations of doctrinal 'modernism' on the part of a few eminent Anglican theological scholars. A group of young men in Oxford had produced a book of essays in which they sought to formulate their theological thinking as a result of what they had recently learnt in the school of 'Greats'. This book, which was entitled *Foundations*, contained an essay by the Reverend B. H. Streeter which seemed to imply that it was possible and defensible for an Anglican to have an open mind on the question of the physical Resurrection of our Lord. At about the same time an old friend of Gore's, Dr Sanday, who was a biblical scholar of international reputation, announced that he could no longer accept the validity of the miracles recorded in the New Testament. The views which he proceeded to publicize amounted to a denial both of the Virgin Birth and of the physical Resurrection of our Lord. These aberrations, added to a recent publication of Dr Hensley Henson (later Bishop of Durham) which seemed to him heretical in its tendencies, saddened and depressed Gore to such an extent that he contemplated resigning his see in his protest. He was dissuaded from doing so only by the urgent pleadings of the Archbishop (Davidson) reinforcing those of his friends Talbot and Scott Holland. Nevertheless he remained deeply disturbed in his mind at the growth of what he regarded as disruptive theological speculation and its consequent danger to faith and morals. He was acutely dissatisfied with the refusal of his brother bishops corporately to face the issues involved, and he felt increasingly that he could more effectively counter the inroads of modernism as a freelance writer, thinker and speaker than as a diocesan bishop hampered at every point by collective episcopal inertia.

The outbreak of war in 1914, however, perforce banished any

thought of immediate resignation, and all through what to him were the nightmare years of armed conflict Gore remained at his post. He twice visited the troops in France, he loyally but without enthusiasm followed his sovereign in eschewing the use of alcohol for the duration, he received the eminent Nonconformist divine, Dr R. H. Campbell, into the Church of England and in 1916 he gave a characteristically vital lead to his diocese in its participation in the 'National Mission of Repentance and Hope'. As Bishop of Oxford he was also Chancellor of the Noble Order of the Garter, and at the outbreak of hostilities he was required to append his signature to documents depriving certain enemy monarchs of their knighthoods. Later in the day he announced with glee, 'I have deposed three Kings!' The greater part of the episcopal palace was turned into a convalescent home for officers and its lovely lawns were ploughed up for the production of vegetables. The results of this latter sacrifice were not highly satisfactory but at least he felt he had made some material contribution to the national war effort.

In June 1918, at the invitation of the government he went to the United States, in company with other eminent religious leaders, to discuss with their American counterparts the Churches' contribution to a new post-war order. He thoroughly enjoyed the experience and was captivated by New York with its exhilarating tempo of life and its mechanical aids to comfortable living. There was nothing, he said, which could not be had at a moment's notice—except tranquillity! He even announced in an expansive moment, his intention of settling in New York after his retirement.

He spoke mainly on the proposed League of Nations and for the necessity, once German militarism had been destroyed, of readmitting Germany to the comity of nations. He also spoke about industrial conditions in England, concerning which he found considerable curiosity in the United States. His public lectures were a tremendous success. He held his audiences enthralled by the originality and profundity of his thought, and one who heard him likened his compulsive power to that of John the Baptist or one of the Old Testament prophets. He discussed politics and religion with President Wilson, visited military camps, gave innumerable interviews to the Press, visited Washington, Chicago, Cleveland (where, at a church service, 'the opening prayer informed the Almighty what I had said!'), and then on to Tennessee, Georgia and Alabama in the Deep South. From thence he returned to the Middle West— Milwaukee, Nashota, Detroit, and then eastwards to Boston. Here he preached four times on the Sunday, including a sermon in Harvard Chapel, one in Trinity Church, and one in the cathedral. Further engagements followed in Washington, Philadelphia, Baltimore and New York and finally, on Monday November 11, as the guns on the Western Front were being silenced, he stepped on board the liner which was to bring him back to a war-weary Europe.

A short time after his return Gore reached the age of 66 and he felt that the time had come to lay down his episcopal burdens and to devote himself, for whatever years might still be granted him, to applying his pen to the great causes which he had at heart—Biblical Scholarship, Church Unity, World Peace, Social Justice and, above all and as a consequence of all, the advancement of God's Kingdom. In March he submitted his resignation to the Archbishop, to take effect on 1 July.

At first there were hopes at Mirfield that Gore might return to Community life, but this he (no doubt wisely) decided against. At his age and with his independence of mind, it would have been virtually impossible for him to adapt himself to monastic conditions of life. He wished, however, to retain his connexion with the Community and applied for election as Prelate Brother, the status granted to members called to the Episcopate by which they could still observe the Rule as it concerned prayer, celibacy and simplicity of life but with otherwise complete freedom of movement and control of personal finance. His election as Prelate Brother having taken place, Gore quietly laid down the reins of office. Free for the first time for seventeen years from episcopal responsibilities, he settled near Oxford Circus in London in a house which he rented from the Vicar and Churchwardens of All Saints' Church, Margaret Street. Various offers of employment had been made to him— the Chair of Theology at King's College, London, a Westminster Canonry, the Mastership of the Temple. But while each of these suggestions had its own particular attraction, the allure of his newly-found freedom proved strongest of all, and, although he was far from rich and drew no pension as a retired diocesan bishop, Gore gratefully declined these various attempts to provide him with an income and a platform.

He found immediate happiness in his new mode of life. After a succession of vast, uncomfortable official residences, he rejoiced in the convenience and comfort of what he called his 'beloved hovel'. Instinctively he preferred simplicity in his mode of living. He liked to travel by public transport, and he had long before adopted the Shavian custom of conducting as much as practicable of his correspondence on postcards. He kept by him a supply of stamped cards with only the words 'Sorry, Can't. C.G.' typed on them, for immediate dispatch in reply to the innumerable requests to speak, preach or lecture which reached him daily. At the same time he enjoyed his new freedom to sample the delights of town. He joined the Royal Societies Club and frequently dined there. The Queen's Hall Promenade Concerts were a great joy to him in their season. He loved, too, to visit the Zoological Gardens, but maintained that he always returned from them an agnostic. He was unable, he said, to comprehend how the Almighty could fit such curious creatures into His moral scheme of things!

In spite of his technical retirement, Gore remained as busy as ever. He preached and spoke regularly up and down the country. He sat on innumerable committees and wrote lengthy letters to the Press on a variety of topics, religious and secular. A deep friendship had sprung up between himself and Archbishop Davidson and Gore frequently supped at Lambeth on Sunday nights. Of his older friends, Scott Holland had died in 1918 and of Talbot he saw little until his retirement from Winchester in 1924. He made hosts of new friends, however, and was always greatly in demand for his warm-hearted sympathy, brilliant conversational powers and (for one of his years) remarkable exuberance.

Late in 1919 Gore joined the staff of King's College as lecturer in theology, and subsequently was elected a Fellow and then a Life Governor. From 1924 to 1928 he was Dean of the Faculty of Theology in the University of London, a position in which his extraordinary gifts of mind and character were put to constant and profitable use. By way of contrast he was licensed as assistant curate of Grosvenor Chapel. This is an extra-parochial place of worship and is attached to Liddon House, an institution fulfilling in London a purpose similar to that of Pusey House in Oxford. Here Gore preached at least once a month and delivered courses of sermons at regular intervals. These two appointments not only provided Gore with regular employment, but they also contributed to his status as 'maid-of-all-work to the Church of England'—his own description of the multifarious tasks and interests for which he found time during this period of so-called retirement. Among the organiza-tions and causes to which he gave active assistance were the Council of Christian Ministers on Social Questions, the Chris-tian Social Crusade, the Industrial Christian Fellowship, the General Council of the League of Nations, the Oxford Mission to Calcutta, the Universities' Mission to Central Africa (of which he had become President in 1917), the Board of Gover-nors of Pusey House, the World Conference on Faith and Order, and the Archbishop's Eastern Churches Committee. At Arch-bishop Davidson's request he also served as a member of the Anglican delegation to the third of the famous Malines Con-ferences held in 1923 to explore the possibilities of reunion between the Church of England and the Church of Rome. Gore had little confidence that these talks would lead to any satis-factory conclusions, the attitude of the Papacy on such fundamental matters as Anglican Orders, biblical criticism, papal authority and infallibility being what they were; and he for one was not surprised when, after the saintly Cardinal Mercier's death in 1926, his successor received instructions from Rome that the Conversations must cease.

His dealings with the Orthodox Churches of the East had a happier outcome. In the spring of 1923 he made a tour of eastern Europe to inform himself of the post-war state of religion generally in that area, as well as to study at first hand the Orthodox Churches in, so to speak, their natural habitat. He visited Prague, Budapest, Bucharest, Belgrade (where he was received by the King and had conversations with the Orthodox Patriarch and other highly-placed ecclesiastics), Sofia and Constantinople. Here he called at the Phanar to pay his respects to the Oecumenical Patriarch, the spiritual head of all the Orthodox Churches, preached at the headquarters of the British Army of Occupation and called on the newly-elected Caliph, Prince Abdul-Mejid. From Turkey Gore went by sea to the Piraeus, visited all the usual sights (including the Acropolis by moonlight) and was also received by King George of Greece. His tour both fascinated and exhausted him. He returned home impressed with Orthodox spirituality and the beauty of Orthodox liturgical worship, but also with a consciousness of the need for disseminating a more widespread knowledge of Anglicanism amongst the Eastern Churches generally. The impression made by Gore himself was summed up by the words of a Serbian student who described him as 'the greatest man we have met', and by a Greek professor who declared, 'His coming among us will not be forgotten.'

Theologically, the last ten years of Gore's life were mainly occupied with defending the Liberal Catholicism which he had held and taught ever since the publication of *Lux Mundi* against on the one hand, Anglo-Catholic extremists who took their doctrines 'all hot from Rome', and, on the other, the Modernists who in Gore's view were reducing Christianity to little more than Unitarianism. Gore, with his consistently anti-Roman position, was the object of deep suspicion and indeed dislike on the part of the extremist clergy and laity who largely dominated the post-war Anglo-Catholic Movement. Nevertheless, such was his tremendous prestige that when the first Anglo-Catholic Congress was brought to a triumphant conclusion with a great mass-meeting in the Albert Hall, not only was Gore invited to address it but his appearance on the platform was the signal for an outburst of prolonged cheering on the part of a vast audience estimated at some thirteen thousand. His speech was so continually interrupted by enthusiastic applause that he was compelled to ask his hearers to withhold their plaudits until the end of each sentence!

Somehow or other, in the midst of all these manifold activities Gore found time for reading and writing, though how he did so appears something of a miracle. He always summarized every important book that he read and made copious notes for future reference. When it came to writing his own books he did so in longhand; he never acquired the habit of dictating to an amanuensis and so unmechanically minded was he that the use of a typewriter would probably have been beyond him. He regarded his writing as his major contribution to contemporary religious thought and practice, and during this period of his life he produced his *Exposition of the Epistles of St John* at which he had been working, on and off, for some twenty years. This work, of which some critics complained that it contained more Gore than John, was followed by his famous trilogy, *Belief in God* (1921), *Belief in Christ* (1922) and *The Holy Spirit and the Church*. This great work was later issued in one volume as *The Reconstruction of Belief*, and was an attempt to restate, in modern terms and in harmony with modern discoveries and critical methods, the faith of the Church as it had been hammered out and held in the first five centuries of primitive Christianity—the faith once delivered to the saints presented in conformity with twentieth-century categories of thought and scientific methods of reasoning. Its dogmas were put to the test of reason and history in a spirit of free inquiry, unhindered by traditional presuppositions or predilections. He laid great stress on God's revelation of Himself to the Old Testament prophets and insisted that the belief in God upon which our Western civilization and our religious beliefs are based derives first from the prophets of Israel and then, and of course more fully, from Jesus of Nazareth. The whole work was a vindication of Christianity searchingly tested at the bar of reason and history. It naturally evoked a considerable measure of criticism, mainly from Modernist quarters, and many of the objections levelled against the three books were dealt with in a further volume entitled *Can We Then Believe?*

In May 1927, Gore moved to a small house in Eaton Terrace, a stone's-throw from the Church of Holy Trinity, Sloane Street, where he celebrated the Holy Eucharist three mornings a week.

He continued to interest himself in the wider affairs of Christendom, and he attended the World Conference on Faith and Order held at Lausanne later that year. Here he firmly maintained the Catholic standpoint on controverted questions such as those relating to the sacraments, but always with an underlying purpose towards genuine reunion based upon sound principles unambiguously propounded. He was convinced of the special opportunities vouchsafed to the Anglican Church to act as a bridge in such matters between the Catholic and Protestant viewpoints.

When the draft of the Revised Prayer Book was published in that same year Gore found that on the whole its contents represented an advance in a Catholic direction considerably beyond what he had dared to hope. There were certain features of the revision which he disliked, notably the rigid insistence that the use of the Reserved Sacrament should be confined strictly to those who were sick. But he could neither understand nor sympathize with the very violent opposition of the more extreme Anglo-Catholics, and he threw all the weight of his influence into getting the book accepted by the Convocations and Parliament. Its subsequent rejection by the Commons in 1927 and again in 1928 Gore accepted with a certain equanimity. He foresaw that this rejection might prove a blessing in disguise, but for the Church itself to have rejected the Bishops' proposal in the Convocations and Church Assembly would have had, in his view, disastrous effects upon Anglican internal harmony.

The following year saw the culmination of many years oi labour when the Society for Promoting Christian Knowledge published *A New Commentary on Holy Scripture*, a tremendous undertaking on the part of a numerous group of Anglican scholars with Gore as general editor. This work, in one volume originally but later published in two parts, contained notes of comment on every book of the Old Testament, New Testament and Apocrypha, as well as a number of admirable essays on a wide range of biblical subjects. The *New Commentary* (frequently referred to as 'Gore's' for convenience) was a notable contribution to Anglican scholarship, and remains still the most useful and up-to-date work of its kind.

B.B.–N*

Other volumes which came from Gore's pen during the next two or three years were *Christ and Society* (1928), lectures delivered under the aegis of the Halley Stewart Trust and dealing with the social implications of the Christian Faith (a subject always near to Gore's heart); *Jesus of Nazareth* (1929), a masterly little study of the person and ministry of our Lord specially written for the Home University Library; and *The Philosophy of The Good Life* (1930), the Gifford Lectures delivered during the previous winter in which Gore reviewed the various philosophic systems by which men have sought to regulate their moral and ethical conduct from Zoroaster to Christ. His last piece of writing, *Reflections on the Litany*, was published the day after he died. It was rich with the stored-up wisdom of a lifetime and, short though it was in length, a precious anthology in itself of Gore's doctrinal and sociological teaching.

Although he was now 77 years of age and had been unwell for most of that autumn, Gore set out in November 1930 for a further visit to India. The objects he had in mind were to see for himself the progress of the Oxford Mission since his previous visit in 1884 and to renew acquaintances made at missionary gatherings in England. He stayed four days in Bombay, visited the Cowley Fathers in Poona, and went on to Calcutta where he made his temporary headquarters with the Oxford Mission. From there he paid flying visits to outlying stations of the Mission, thoroughly enjoying the heat and the varied scenery, delivering innumerable sermons and lectures, dashing up to Darjeeling—'for a lark', as he explained in a letter to a friend—and then returning to Calcutta to preach at the Mission's Jubilee celebrations and to conduct the Community's annual retreat. It was a programme which in that climate would have exhausted many a man of half his years. He stayed for a week at Delhi as the guest of the Viceroy, Lord Irwin,[1] where he was a tremendous success with the junior members of the Vice-regal staff, and where he was also able to visit the Cambridge Mission.

Then he was off to South India, to Travancore and Madras, where he made strenuous but mostly unsuccessful efforts to

[1] Later first Earl of Halifax, K.G., (*ob.* 1959).

mediate in a long-standing dispute between two contending factions in the ancient Syrian ('Mar Thoma') Church of Malabar. He included Nasik in his itinerary, in order to confer with Bishop Loyd on the South Indian reunion scheme, and then on to Bombay to re-embark for home. He arrived there, in intense heat, sick and exhausted and suffered a collapse from which, however, he recovered sufficiently to board his ship. He arrived back in England early in May, on a Saturday. The following day he insisted on celebrating the Eucharist at Holy Trinity, Sloane Street, but collapsed at the altar and had to be assisted to the vestry.

Medical examination revealed nothing organically wrong, but during the months which followed he was forced to recognize the limitations imposed by his age and by years of unsparing labour. He still preached from time to time; he continued to read voraciously and to take the keenest interest in public affairs. Towards the end of the summer, however, the strain of his Indian tour began to take its toll. He was forced to give up all his activities, and began to feel himself a sick man. In January of the following year (1932) he attended a meeting in London to bid farewell to the newly-appointed Bishop of Labuan and Sarawak. He sat huddled in his chair and looked miserably ill. A few days later he developed a severe cough and had to be moved to a nursing home. Pneumonia was diagnosed and he realized that the end was near. On the Friday he was still able to sit up in bed scribbling postcards to one or two close friends. That night the Archbishop of Canterbury visited him and found him in a semi-conscious condition. Twice the Archbishop heard him murmur 'Transcendant Glory' before he again relapsed into a state of coma. He died on the morning of Sunday, 17 January 1932.

His body lay in state before the high altar in Holy Trinity, Sloane Street, and an immense crowd of people from every walk of life filed in to take their last farewell. On the following day, after a Solemn Requiem sung by Bishop Frere of Truro, one of the original members of the Community of the Resurrection, his body was cremated. The ashes were taken to Mirfield where they were laid to rest before the high altar of the

Community church. A stone slab marking the spot bears the simple inscription: '*Carolus Gore. Episcopus. Fundator*'. It is as nobly fitting in its brevity as those which mark the last resting places of St Patrick and St Cuthbert.

At a memorial service held in Westminster Abbey and attended by the bishops and clergy of the Convocation of Canterbury, the Archbishop gave thanks for 'Charles Gore, bishop, scholar, thinker, teacher, prophet and saint'. In a memorial sermon preached in Christ Church Cathedral, Oxford, the Regius Professor, Dr H. L. Goudge, paid the University's tribute to one of its greatest sons. 'It is a sorrow to have lost him', he said, 'but not an overwhelming sorrow, for his work was done. God lent him to us for seventy-nine years, and that was much longer than we deserved.'

Gore was mourned by men and women all over the country —and far beyond its bounds—by people of widely differing religious views, and by many who held none at all. However they chose to express their veneration, however they may have differed from him on specific issues, all who had been brought into close personal contact with him revered him as a saint. It was a great Nonconformist scholar who said of him, 'I always felt that he was the most Christlike Christian I knew.'

Charles Gore stands in the great succession of Anglican divines, worthy to be numbered among such as Cranmer, Hooker, Andrewes, Laud, Cosin, Ken, Butler, Keble, Pusey, Liddon and King. Great scholars, pastors, teachers; devoted sons of *Ecclesia Anglicana*; servants of God and lights of their respective generations. He was the twentieth century embodiment of all that is highest and best in Anglican thought and piety, oecumenical in the wideness of his outlook, orthodox in theology yet never despising the God-given faculty of reason. He was a great Catholic Christian whose affinities were worldwide, universal; at one with the thinkers and teachers and holy men of the Church of all the ages.

It is more than a quarter of a century since he was taken from us and a generation has arisen who never saw that tall, angular figure, that ascetic face with the nobly-domed head, the fiercely-jutting beard; who never saw him wriggling and twisting his long limbs into incredible convolutions as he wrestled with some knotty point of faith or morals; who never heard that resonant voice proclaim, 'I am pro-foundly convinced. . . .'

Yet his influence remains; his work endures. Anglicanism today is very much what Gore made it. Its theological habits of thought are those which he expounded with such force and clarity. Its attitude to social questions it has largely learned from such books as *The Sermon on the Mount* and *Christ and Society*. Its sacramental teaching approximates ever more closely to his own as he proclaimed it in *The Body of Christ*. The great Religious Community which he founded continues to flourish, and to serve God and His Church at home and overseas. Of few could it ever more truly have been said that 'he, being dead, yet speaketh'.

BIBLIOGRAPHY

THOMAS CRANMER

Biography, J. Strype, London, 1694.
Modern Lives, H. J. Todd (2 vols.) London, 1831. C. H. Callette, A. J. Mason, A. D. Innes, A. F. Pollard, C. H. Smyth, A. C. Deane, and Hilaire Belloc.
Cranmer and the Reformation, Canon F. E. Hutchinson (1951).
Article in *Dictionary of National Biography*, J. Gairdner, 1888.
Works: The Remains of Thomas Cranmer, ed. H. Jenkyns (4 vols.) Oxford, 1833.
Miscellaneous Writings and Letters, ed. E. Cox, Parker Society, 1846.
Writings and Disputations . . . Relative to the Sacrament of the Lord's Supper, ed. E. Cox, Parker Society, 1844.

RICHARD HOOKER

Works, ed. J. Keble (3 vols.) 1836.
Life by Izaak Walton, 1665, reprinted in Keble's edition of the *Works*.
An Introduction to the Fifth Book of Hooker's Treatise of the Laws of Ecclesiastical Polity, F. Paget, 1899.
Richard Hooker, L. S. Thornton, C. R., 1924.
The Judicious Marriage of Mr Hooker and the Birth of the Laws of Ecclesiastical Polity, C. J. Sisson, 1940.
Richard Hooker and Contemporary Political Ideas, F. J. Shirley, 1949.
The Place of Hooker in the History of Thought, P. Munz, 1952.
Article in *Dictionary of National Biography*, S. Lee, 1891.

THOMAS KEN

The Prose Works of Thomas Ken, D.D., and a Short Account of his Life, W. Hoskins, Esq. The whole collected by J. T. Round, 1838.
Lives, W. T. Bowles (2 vols.), London, 1830. *A Layman*, J. L. Anderdon (2 vols.), London, 1851. E. H. Plumptre (2 vols.), 1878. F. A. Clarke, 1896. H. A. L. Rice, 1958.
Article in *Dictionary of National Biography*, W. Hunt, 1892.
Thomas Ken and Izaak Walton, E. Marston, 1908.
The Non-Jurors, J. H. Overton, 1902.
The High Church Schism, J. W. C. Wand, 1951.

WILLIAM LAW

The Life and Opinions of the Rev. Wm. Law, A.M., J. H. Overton.

William Law, Non-Juror and Mystic, J. H. Overton, 1881.

William Law and Eighteenth Century Quakerism, S. H. Hobhouse, 1927.

About William Law, A. W. Hopkinson (S.P.C.K.), 1848.

Memorials of the Birthplace and Residence of the Rev. William Law, M.A., at King's Cliffe, in Northamptonshire, 'Published for Mr G. Moreton, by the London Printing Works, Guildford, Surrey', 1892–3.

Selected Mystical Writings of William Law, S. H. Hobhouse, 1938.

William Law, a Neglected Master of English Prose, H. Tallen, 1948.

Articles in *D.N.B.* and *Oxford Dictionary of the Christian Church.*

THOMAS BRAY

The Reverend Thomas Bray, E. L. Pennington, Church Historical Society, Philadelphia, 1934.

Thomas Bray, 1658–1730, John Wolfe Lydekker, D.D. (Church Historical Society, Philadelphia, 1942).

Thomas Bray, H. P. Thompson (S.P.C.K.), 1954.

Church and State in England in the Eighteenth Century, N. Sykes, D.D., 1934.

Article in *Dictionary of English Church History,* J. H. Overton, 1886.

Article in *Dictionary of English Church History,* W. H. Hutton, D.D. (Mowbray, 3rd Edition, 1948).

A Short History of the English Church, C. P. S. Clarke (Mowbray, new edition, 1948).

Eighteenth Century Piety, W. K. Lowther Clarke, S.D., 1944.

THOMAS WILSON

Life and Works, C. Cruttwell (2 vols.), London, 1781.

Life of Thomas Wilson, H. Stowell, 1819.

Works, Library of Anglo-Catholic Theology (7 vols.) with *Life,* John Keble (1847–63).

Articles in *D.N.B.* and *The Oxford Dictionary of the Christian Church.*

JOHN MASON NEALE

Memoir by Eleanor A. Towle, 1906.

Selections from the Writings of John Mason Neale, ed. Lawson, London, 1910.

Articles in *D.N.B.* and *Oxford Dictionary of the Christian Church.*

NATHANIEL WOODARD

Life, Sir John Otter, London, 1925.
The Story of the Woodard Schools, K. E. Kirk, Abbey Press, 1953.
Articles in *D.N.B.* and *Oxford Dictionary of the Christian Church.*

CHARLES GORE

Life of Charles Gore, G. L. Prestige, 1935.
Charles Gore, G. Crosse, 1932.
Edward Stuart Talbot and Charles Gore, A. Mansbridge, 1935.
Gore: A Study in Liberal Catholic Thought, James Carpenter, Faith Press, 1960.
Articles in *D.N.B.* and *Oxford Dictionary of the Christian Church.*